Homegrown

The New Age of Terrorism

Dr. Robert Brzenchek and Dr. Sean Blinn

First Edition

Keystone College

King's College

Bassim Hamadeh, CEO and Publisher
John Remington, Managing Executive Editor
Gem Rabanera, Senior Project Editor
Susana Christie, Senior Developmental Editor
Rachel Kahn, Production Editor
Asfa Arshi, Graphic Design Assistant
Kylie Bartolome, Licensing Associate
Natalie Piccotti, Director of Marketing
Kassie Graves, Senior Vice President, Editorial
Jamie Giganti, Director of Academic Publishing

Printed in the United States of America.

Contents

Acknowledgments

Robert Brzenchek would like to acknowledge the men and women he served alongside in our law enforcement and military ranks to protect and serve citizens throughout the United States against foreign and domestic enemies. In addition, he would like to acknowledge all those who support his efforts to raise global awareness of terrorism.

Sean Blinn would like to acknowledge the dedicated professionals who have worked tirelessly to protect our homeland. He is eternally grateful for those who have provided him with the opportunities and experiences that have shaped him as a person. From his parents' influences to the colleagues who have contributed to his academic and professional success, he has been truly blessed with all of their support.

CHAPTER 1

Terrorism Defined

For every targeted threat, we need at least three options: kinetic, cyber (offensive and defensive), & counter threat finance.

—Director of Operations, United States Special Operations Command

GUIDING QUESTIONS

- How has the terrorism designation impacted federal and state statutes?
- Why do various United States governmental agencies differ in their definition of terrorism?
- What are the key definitional characteristics of the term "terrorism"?

INTRODUCTION

Before we begin our examination of domestic terrorism and how it impacts various areas of societal functions, we must appreciate the complexity of how the term "terrorism" is defined. In many cases, this term has been assigned to describe a multitude of events that are associated with violence, and many people struggle with distinguishing between what is criminalistic and what is terroristic. Interestingly, the assignment of this term can be used in a variety of ways, and the use of this term can be based on that user's understanding of the term. There are many cases, as observed in various media outlets and presented by high-profile commentators, when their understanding of terrorism is not entirely accurate. It is critical to use the correct meaning of the term since this will prevent confusion regarding what qualifies as terrorism.

KEY TERMS

- terrorism
- tactic
- strategy
- random terror
- tactical terror

TERRORISM DEFINED

For us to really develop an understanding of terrorism, we have to examine how this term is used by various organizations and governments—to include its statutory definitions. As indicated in the following passages, we are going to evaluate the various differences in how terrorism is defined. As a variety of definitions will be presented, you will find a variety of consistent characteristics that are attached to each definition. These characteristics help shape our understanding of what terrorism really is.

First, let us examine a basic definition of terrorism. According to Oxford University Press (n.d.), **terrorism** is defined as "the calculated use of violence or threat of violence to inculcate fear. Terrorism is intended to coerce or intimidate governments or societies in the pursuit of goals that are generally political, religious, or ideological." This definition presents a lean illustration of some important characteristics that go into the qualification of the term. While we can almost universally associate violence with a terroristic act, pay close attention to the explanation of why terrorism occurs: The focus is to achieve goals that are either political, religious, or ideological in nature. Essentially, this definition presents the argument that those who commit terrorism focus on creating change in societies (a macrolevel impact) by a violent intervention directed toward how society's institutions operate. With this understanding, we can rule out the typical criminal behavior committed by those offenders who engage in violent acts that are self-serving at the individual level as an act that meets the qualification standards of terrorism.

Now that we have clarified that terrorism is focused on systematic change within governments and/or societies, it is essential to understand how the U.S. government defines domestic terrorism at the federal statutory level. According to the Anti-Terrorism Clarification Act of 2018, domestic terrorism is defined by activities that involve acts that are dangerous to human life that are a violation of the criminal laws of the United States or of any state. Additionally, these activities are intended to intimidate or coerce a civilian population, to influence the policy of a government by intimidation or coercion, or to affect the conduct of a government by mass destruction, assassination, or kidnappings within the territorial jurisdiction of the United States. If we examine the definition of domestic terrorism, it is clear there are some variations in how terrorism is defined under the domestic characterization as opposed to what was described by Oxford. To further understand how domestic terrorism is defined by governmental organizations, let's review some of those definitions that help shape the defensive and offensive strategies when addressing this particular threat.

THE FEDERAL BUREAU OF INVESTIGATION

As noted by the Federal Bureau of Investigation (FBI, 2010), the National Defense Authorization Act (an annual bill that guides policies and funding of U.S. defense agencies) requires the FBI, the Department of Homeland Security, and the Director of National

Intelligence to work together to develop standard definitions of terminology relating to domestic terrorism and uniform methodologies for tracking events that meet the criteria for domestic terrorism. This collaboration is focused on developing standardized definitions and ensuring that the language used in each definition is accepted and used uniformly across other agencies. As noted by Pascus (2019), the FBI identifies domestic terrorism as being limited to activities that occur in the United States, where political, religious, social, racial, or environmental issues can trigger acts of violence.

TACTICS AND STRATEGIES

Another topic area that requires some additional terms and definitions involves explaining how tactics and strategies exist in domestic terrorist operations. When the term "tactic" is used, we must understand that this is quite different from the other term, "strategy." A **tactic** is a unique action that is meant to influence or create a response that contributes toward a successful strategy. For example, if a domestic terrorist group seeks to prevent abortion clinics from operating within a geographic area, they can help influence this by engaging in violent acts. One tactic they could use is to detonate a homemade bomb that destroys a local abortion clinic building. The tactic here is the bombing of a building. A **strategy** (or strategic goal), as observed within the context of terrorism, is a plan comprised of one or more goals that work toward a desired outcome. Continuing with the abortion clinic example, the terrorist would achieve their strategic goal if they could influence other abortion clinics to cease their operations through fear of injury.

A DOMESTIC AND INTERNATIONAL PERSPECTIVE

When categorizing what constitutes a terrorist act, it is helpful to turn to the federal government's definition. By statute, terrorism is "premeditated, politically motivated violence perpetrated against noncombatant targets by subnational groups or clandestine agents" (Latiff, 2018). Terrorism can strike anywhere and is a problem beyond New York City (NYC) and Washington, D.C. (D.C). Symbolic targets exist throughout the United States, such as federal buildings and Jewish synagogues.

Why the United States? Why not? As evidenced by past terroristic events around the country—such as the Fort Hood shooting in Killeen, Texas, and the drive-by shooting at a U.S. military recruiting office in Little Rock, Arkansas—terrorism can strike anywhere. According to Louis Klarevas (2011), there were 105 terrorist attacks in the United States between 9/11 and the end of 2010, resulting in a combined 27 deaths. The threat within the United States comes mainly from guns, incendiary devices, and instruments of transportation.

What about bombs and weapons of mass destruction (WMDs)? Well, not so much. Since Timothy McVeigh attacked the federal building in Oklahoma City in 1995, the consistent availability of enough fertilizer able to inflict a massive explosion has been strictly prohibited.

Moreover, the likelihood of a terrorist organization acquiring, assembling, and delivering a WMD of any kind is practically unthinkable.

Since 9/11, ecoterrorists have been responsible for most attacks inside the United States. Environmental and animal rights groups were responsible for 53 attacks of the 105 domestic attacks compiled in the Klarevas data set. Meanwhile, jihadists have attacked within the United States 13 times since 9/11 (Klarevas, 2011). There are three factors, however, that allow jihadist attacks to stand out as the most troubling: (a) jihadist attacks account for most of the fatalities inflicted here at home; (b) jihadist attacks are often perpetrated by lone wolfs, making their early detection more difficult given the lack of preoperational "chatter"; (c) most jihadist attacks have occurred in the last 3 years, indicating a significant rise in this type of threat (Klarevas, 2011).

Will the United States be a likely target for terrorists? Probably not. Can an attack be ruled out? Definitely not. The data clearly show that terrorism is driven by a variety of motives, and even if jihadists don't strike in the United States, others might. This point is particularly disconcerting when one takes into consideration the fact that the weapons of choice for domestic terrorists—guns, incendiary devices, and modes of transportation—are all readily available in the United States as well as pretty much everywhere else throughout the globe.

RANDOM AND TACTICAL TERROR

In November 2003, a U.S. military transport plane carrying soldiers engaged in peacekeeping and nation-building in postwar Iraq was shot down by a surface-to-air missile, killing 16 soldiers who were being transported to planes for the first leg of their journey home for a brief leave (Latiff, 2018). Iraqi groups seeking to force the United States out of their country claimed responsibility for the attack. This was a terrorist act. Committing an act causing serious damage to a public transportation system, a telecommunications system, or to any infrastructure that has a public benefit is a terrorist act called **random terror**. It involves placing explosives where people gather—such as post offices, railroads, and airlines—to destroy whoever happens to be there.

On March 30, 1981, at 2:27 p.m., President Ronald Reagan was shot in the chest by a gunman (Latiff, 2018). The would-be assassin, John W. Hinckley, Jr., shot the president as he walked to his limousine after addressing the American Federation of Labor and Congress of Industrial Organizations (AFL-CIO) meeting at the Washington, D.C. Hilton Hotel. Shooting from a distance of about 10 feet, Hinckley shot Reagan, Press Secretary James Brady, Secret Service Agent Timothy J. McCarthy, and Washington policeman Thomas K. Delahanty. Evidence at the subsequent trial indicated that Hinckley was motivated by a desire to impress actress Jodie Foster. In this case, it is a terrorist act called tactical terror (revolutionary). It is called tactical terror because someone committed an act of violence, or committed any act causing harm to [a person's] life, or serious harm to [a person's] body, or

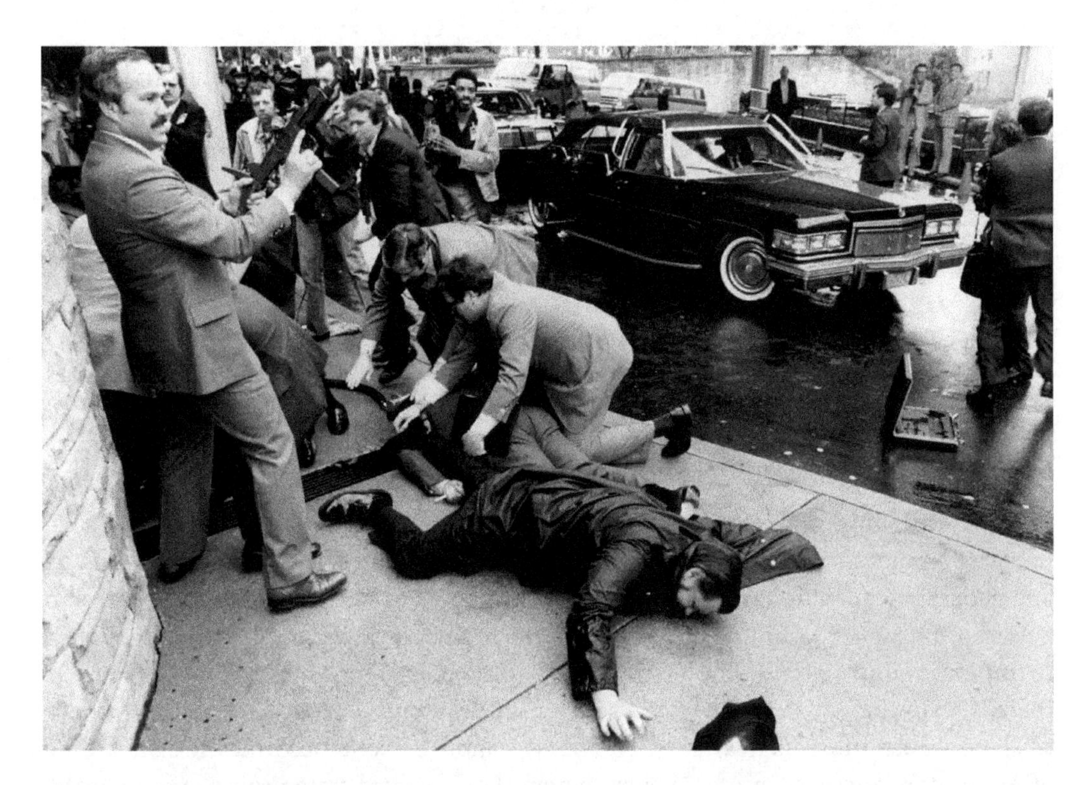

FIGURE 1.1 Hinckley's Assassination Attempt on President Ronald Reagan

the liberty of any person. **Tactical terror** is directed solely against the ruling government as a part of a "broad revolutionary strategic plan" (Latiff, 2018).

Another act of tactical terror occurred just before dawn on October 23, 1983, when a suicide vehicle laden with about 21,000 pounds of TNT blew up the U.S. Marine headquarters near the Beirut, Lebanon, airport (Latiff, 2018). Around 307 persons were reported killed, most of them as they slept (Latiff, 2018). The Free Islamic Revolutionary Movement claimed responsibility for the action. Again, the tactical terror act was a result of the person committing an act causing damage to the property of any state, or of any person, or to the environment, which has caused or is likely to cause significant economic damage. Since this act was committed with the intention to threaten or to compel the government, a foreign government, or an international organization to do or abstain from doing the act, which will cause serious damage or from causing disorder by creating widespread fear among the public, [then] that person has committed a terrorist act.

In April 1999, an attack by two students at Columbine High School in a suburb of Denver, Colorado, resulted in the deaths of 13 and wounded more than 20 people, some of them critically (Latiff, 2018). The attackers—identified as Eric Harris, 18, and Dylan Klebold, 17, both seniors at the school—reportedly laughed and hooted as they opened fire on classmates after having booby-trapped the school with pipe bombs. Harris and Klebold were members of a group calling itself the Trench-coat Mafia, outcasts who bragged about guns and bombs and hated Blacks, Hispanics, and student-athletes.

This is a terrorist act called focused random terror. Focused *random terror* restricts the placing of explosives, for example, to where significant agents of oppression are likely to gather. In this case, the terrorist dislikes Blacks, Hispanics, and student-athletes. Terrorist acts come in all forms and shapes. You never really know why terrorists do the things that they do.

Al-Qaeda and ISIS-led global terrorist warfare are the most dangerous threats ever mounted against humankind. The following paragraphs demonstrate seven characteristics of terrorists, all of which are features of these two organizations as well:

1. NO GEOGRAPHICAL OR NATIONAL RESTRAINTS

The first distinguishing trait of terrorist groups is the influence exerted by transnational terrorist groups such as al Al-Qaeda and ISIS and its affiliates, which are not bound by any geographical or national restraints. Unlike the Cold War's bipolar confrontation between the Soviet Union and the United States, such terrorist groups are not subject to any state control, rendering them virtually unmanageable by world leaders because there is no locality from which to focus defensive or offensive tactics in order to deter or retaliate against subsequent attacks. This became more evident following the dismantling of Al-Qaeda's sanctuary in Afghanistan, where they received state protection under the former Taliban regime. Today, Al-Qaeda and ISIS and its affiliates are dispersed in many lands, especially in lawless regions, including, but not limited to, Pakistan's Waziristan province, Somalia, and Lebanon, where local governments are too weak to assert control over their activities.

2. INTERNATIONAL IN SCOPE AND REACH

Terrorism by Al-Qaeda and ISIS and its affiliates is international in scope and reach. Today no state is geographically immune to transnational terrorism, which can strike against any nation's citizens whether overseas or at home. An example is the Al-Qaeda-affiliated Jemaah Islamiyah (JI) group attack on the JW Marriott and Ritz-Carlton hotels in Jakarta, Indonesia; on July 17, 2009, nine persons were killed and as many as 50 people injured (including eight U.S. citizens) by simultaneous suicide bombings (Latiff, 2018). The bomb at the JW Marriott was detonated at 8:45 a.m. in a restaurant on the ground floor, and the bomb at the Ritz-Carlton was detonated 10 minutes later on the third floor of the restaurant (Latiff, 2018). Another example of the portability of terrorism is the attack against Israeli tourists in Mombasa, Kenya, in November 2002. Three suicide bombers drove an SUV onto the lobby steps of the seaside resort Paradise Hotel and detonated a bomb that killed 13 and injured 80 (Latiff, 2018). This example helps illustrate how a nation's citizens are not immune to terrorist attacks when they travel overseas. (Instructors can utilize any examples/case studies deemed appropriate.) Equally, a neutral country such as Switzerland, which has been proven to be utilized as a transient route by Al-Qaeda operatives prior to 9/11, is another example of how any nation, despite political or religious impartiality, can be exploited by terrorists as they pursue their goals.

Moreover, the fact that geographical distance has lost its significance in today's terrorist environment is further illustrated by three examples. First, some of the Mujahidin who fought against the Soviet troops in the 1980s started in Afghanistan, where they formed Al-Qaeda's nucleus, a second group returned to their countries of origin, where many of them joined radical Islamist movements such as al-Gama'a al-Islammiyya in Egypt or formed new terrorist groupings in other countries. However, when governments, such as Egypt, expelled these returnees, some of them succeeded in being granted tourist visas to the United States. For instance, it was in the U.S. where Sheikh Omar Abdel-Rahman, the blind Egyptian radical cleric, was given a tourist visa in July 1990 as a result of a bureaucratic error, despite having been previously imprisoned in Egypt for terrorist activities (Latiff, 2018). A core group of followers of Sheikh Abdel-Rahman was responsible for the first bombings of the World Trade Center in New York City in February 1993.

In a second example, Muhammad Atta, an Al-Qaeda operative and one of the leaders of the 9/11 plot, left his affluent home in Egypt to study architecture in Hamburg, Germany. While in Hamburg, Atta became radicalized and was recruited into Al-Qaeda. He subsequently attended Al-Qaeda training camps in Afghanistan before returning to Germany and then the United States for the 9/11 attacks.

The new phenomenon of "homegrown" terrorism is another example of how geographical distance has lost its significance in today's transnational terrorist environment. According to precepts of radical Islam, the operatives that engage in terrorism, such as Osama bin Laden and Muhammed Atta, no longer have to originate in the countries or regions controlled by Islam, but now spring from countries and areas where radicals perceive as their "war zone." Examples of terror planned by homegrown terrorists include the suicide bombings in July 2005 by British Islamist extremists against London's transportation system; the discovery in November 2005 of a terrorist cell in Toronto, Canada, that included a former instructor in making bombs at an Al-Qaeda training camp in Afghanistan; and the discovery in May 2007 of a plot by local terrorist "wanna-be's" to attack soldiers at Ft. Dix, New Jersey. Thus, every nation, whether perceived as a potential target or used for logistical purposes, now finds itself situated in "the eye of the storm."

3. EXPERIENCE ON THE BATTLEFIELD

The third characteristic is Al-Qaeda and ISIS experience on the battlefield (Latiff, 2018). Many of Al-Qaeda's and ISIS's operatives have gained valuable experience in insurgent warfare through campaigns with the Soviets in Afghanistan, consequent combat training in Al-Qaeda's training camps (under Taliban auspices), and in the insurgent warfare in Iraq. This characteristic differentiates them from their terrorist predecessors, many of whom were affluent students and intellectuals, insulated from war.

4. MOTIVATION

The fourth characteristic is their motivation, which is transnational in its ambition and scope (Latiff, 2018). Unlike their terrorist predecessors who were motivated by political or socioeconomic grievances that were localized and amenable to compromise, Al-Qaeda and ISIS and terrorists influenced and/or affiliated with Al-Qaeda and ISIS see themselves as embarking on a mission to fulfill God's divine command to establish a caliphate that will unite radical Islamic ideals and rule the world—with no room for negotiation or compromise.

Bin Laden and his coterie understand that they are incapable of conquering the world immediately, so their objective will be accomplished in two stages. The first stage is centered on the gradual collapse of Arab and Muslim governments by undermining their stability through terrorist subversion. This is why most of Al-Qaeda and ISIS attacks occur in Arab and Muslim countries such as Algeria, Egypt, Jordan, Turkey, Saudi Arabia, Pakistan, Iraq, and Indonesia. The Arab and Muslim governments will also be undermined, in Al-Qaeda and ISIS's view, by forcing the United States to withdraw its troops from Arab lands, influencing the West to cease economically supporting these regimes and pressuring the West, and especially America, to become isolationist and withdraw from Middle Eastern affairs. According to their perceived calculations, governments such as those in Jordan, Egypt, and Saudi Arabia will collapse without American support.

Al-Qaeda's and ISIS's methodical strategy will progress from the stage of instability to a second stage—the establishment of the Islamic caliphate. Al-Qaeda perceived the catastrophic impact of the 9/11 attacks as a rally to Muslims around the world to rise up against their regimes. In their view, the implementation of their tactical plan's first stage will shake the confidence of Islamic regimes worldwide. Accordingly, the Al-Qaeda and ISIS-led conflict against the West is not a war between religions, such as between Islam and Christianity; instead, the war is between radical Islam and the rest of the world, including mainstream Islam. It is the Islamic extremists, for example, who refer to their coreligionists as infidels. It is important for us to understand this phenomenon, a war within the religion of Islam because the burden for response is first and foremost the responsibility of the Muslims themselves. It is up to them to save Islam from the radical Islamists.

5. INTEREST IN DEPLOYING WEAPONS OF MASS DESTRUCTION

The fifth characteristic is the interest of Al-Qaeda and ISIS and its affiliates in employing weapons of mass destruction (WMD), which represents a transition from conventional to nonconventional terrorism (Latiff, 2018). Al-Qaeda and ISIS and their affiliates have the motivation and operational capability to deploy certain WMD weapons and devices, as demonstrated by the WMD "cookbooks" and manuals found on their Internet sites (Latiff, 2018). Al-Qaeda and ISIS possess the motivation—but perhaps not the operational capability—to employ nuclear weapons. Bin Laden stated that it is a "sin" not to defend Islam and the rights of Muslims at all costs, even if many Muslims may be hurt by an attack, whether with a conventional weapon or a WMD (Latiff, 2018). There have also been concrete operational plots by Al-Qaeda and ISIS and its affiliates to launch chemical warfare, exemplified by the plot thwarted by Jordanian authorities in April 2004 to use chemical weapons in a series of simultaneous attacks in that country, as well as the waves of chlorine gas attacks that take place in Iraq. The potential to resort to chemical warfare is real and imminent.

6. NONRATIONAL DECISION-MAKING PROCESS

The sixth characteristic of Al-Qaeda and ISIS that makes them so lethal is their "nonrational" decision-making process, coupled with their conception of time (Latiff, 2018). Such decision-making "rationality" is different from Western cost-benefit analysis because it is not rooted in immediate gain or loss considerations, with life on earth not as significant, for example, and life in post-death "paradise" considered an ideal goal (Latiff, 2018). Moreover, short-term military setbacks are not important because they are waging a "100 years" war in which they will ultimately prevail, no matter how many years it will take them to achieve their objectives (Latiff, 2018). Understanding such rationale and cost-benefit analysis is crucial because it demonstrates why it is so difficult to communicate, negotiate, threaten, or deter such groups; whatever message is sent will be interpreted differently by them. Decision-making processes by such terrorist groups pose a greater danger than dealing with past terrorist groups that were amenable to the give-and-take of negotiation and compromise.

7. ORGANIZATION

The final characteristic is organization (Latiff, 2018). Over the years, Al-Qaeda's and ISIS's organizational structure has changed from a structured, hierarchical organization prior to 9/11, with a decision-making process based on command-and-control principles, into the current flat and cellular organizational structure. This organizational change was created by their loss of infrastructure and training bases in Afghanistan and points beyond, which severely hampered their ability to move freely. As a result, Al-Qaeda and ISIS framework evolved from a "central" approach into reliance on other Islamic terrorist organizations as proxies to carry out their operations (Latiff, 2018). Thus, the initiation of an attack might come from Al-Qaeda and ISIS, but its execution might be conducted by others. Today, Al-Qaeda and ISIS rely on their ability to inspire others by utilizing cyberspace to incite and indoctrinate new activists and homegrown terrorists. In this way, Al-Qaeda and ISIS have been able to rely on a new generation of terrorists, many of whom are homegrown.

SUMMARY

Because adolescent males lack male capital, they believe they are disenfranchised and wish to be franchised with male capital wherever they can be honored and revered for masculine behavior. Whether Al-Qaeda, ISIS, or gangs, these are a franchise that allow adolescent males to be loved, honored, and rewarded with hard work, even if the work is deviant and criminal. For example, the gang MS-13, a very large transnational gang, and their leaders are good at recruiting male adolescents because MS-13 draws on a mythic notion of community. In the MS-13's community, called the el barrio (the neighborhood), young adolescent males are inspired—adolescent males who come from disenfranchised families and are drawn to what MS-13 can offer (United States Department of Justice, 2017). Disenfranchised adolescent males who join MS-13 have a place they can obtain positive and negative protection and nurture, socialize, and bond with one another and find leadership from older male role models, which were absent in their lives (United States Department of Justice, 2017). By joining MS-13, adolescent males can also obtain power and wealth that furthers their ideal of being a man. This concept is applied to today's homegrown terrorists.

REVIEW QUESTIONS

Directions: Based on what you have learned in this chapter, respond to the questions and prompts below.

1. Does compliance with standards and laws protect a business and its executives from terrorism liability?
2. What education is appropriate to prepare a professional to face today's terrorism threats?
3. What is the estimated annual economic loss caused by terrorism?

FIGURE CREDITS

Fig. 1.1: Source: https://commons.wikimedia.org/wiki/File:Photograph_of_chaos_outside_the_Washington_Hilton_Hotel_after_the_assassination_attempt_on_President_Reagan_(white_border_removed).png.

CHAPTER 2

A Road to Extremism

GUIDING QUESTIONS

- What is a belief system?
- How do ideologies develop, and why are they difficult to change?
- Is extremism a manifestation of mental illness, or is it caused by deeply held beliefs based on a warped perception of the world?

INTRODUCTION

When we think of terrorism or terroristic acts, we find ourselves envisioning horrific scenarios that make us wonder how a human being engages in such behavior. These scenarios can involve mass shootings, public beheadings, bombings, stabbings, and assassinations. Without a doubt, this type of behavior is unwelcome in any modern society. However, these events occur, and when we watch them on the news or online, we always ask ourselves the same questions: Are these people evil? Are these people mentally ill? What drives a person or group to commit such atrocities? To understand the motivations behind this violent behavior, we must first understand the basics of our psychology.

KEY TERMS

- radicalization
- extremism
- belief system
- ideology
- grievance

OUR BELIEF SYSTEM

When we are born into this world, we are bombarded by a significant amount of information that begins to contribute to the development of how we see the world and where we fit in it.

From the time we are newborns, our brains goes through various developmental stages that allow us to form our intellectual and cognitive abilities. As we engage in regular interactions with influential people in our lives, we begin to develop a **belief system**. Think about the time you spent with your family members as a child. What happened during this period of your life? You were required to follow your parents' rules, and most of your life experiences depended on the extent to which your parents would allow you to explore the world. As a child, depending on the characteristics of your family, you were exposed to a variety of influences that helped shape you as a person. Some of these influences came from religious beliefs, the interpretation of what right and wrong are, the treatment of others, and the value of honesty. Over time, these influences help develop your belief system.

While belief systems are an essential part of who we are, this system is far from being infallible, nor is it something that aligns with the universally accepted beliefs of a society. According to Lewis (2018), beliefs represent a set of parameters constructed within our brain that allows us to understand the world and how we fit in it. With this, Lewis argues that our brain is highly predictive when evaluating and categorizing large amounts of information; moreover, we tend to perceive things that are more aligned with our belief system. Interestingly, as we use our beliefs to help shape our understanding of things, we tend to find ourselves predicting outcomes or perceiving aspects of life in an error-prone manner (Lewis, 2018). This helps explain why some people or groups will present a fierce opposition to controversial pieces of public policy (e.g., the ongoing debate over abortion practices in the United States).

UNDERSTANDING IDEOLOGY

According to Cambridge University Press's (n.d.) online dictionary, the term **ideology** is defined as "a set of beliefs or principles, especially one on which a political system, party, or organization is based." Notice that Cambridge's definition does not include the word "logic." The development of a person's ideology has not been privy to a strict assessment that is based on the principles of validity; actually, an ideology is a flexible set of beliefs formed through various influences that make sense to the person. However, there are many instances where a person's ideological position on something is very rigid and represents a lack of desire to understand an opposing ideological viewpoint. In fact, some individual and group ideologies are so toxic and so misaligned that society has determined them to be a threat; we call this an "extremist ideology."

An extremist ideology takes hold of a person's personality for many reasons. Some of the core influences for **extremism** are rooted in the way people view their (a) economic status, (b) religious beliefs, and (c) political views. In most cases, these categories are the foundation for a person's life, and when others threaten their tenets, the potential for violent extremism can develop through a process of radicalization. However, many members of our society present with a variety of risk factors that can make them susceptible to joining extremist groups. For individuals who feel disconnected or removed from any community-level acceptance, an extremist group can help them find purpose or a sense of belonging. We can see younger members of society joining extremist organizations that align with neo-Nazism. Other societal members could develop extremist views if they perceive public policy or governmental actions as being unjust or dangerous to that person's belief system. As Youngblood (2020) explains, *radicalization* is a process that nurtures extremism through a variety of environmental factors. An excellent example of this can be observed with how Timothy McVeigh expressed his grievances against the Ruby Ridge shootout and the tragedy that occurred at the Branch Davidian compound in Waco, Texas. We will further explore McVeigh's radicalization process in Chapter 8.

ECONOMIC INFLUENCE

Through mere observation, we can conclude that our society is composed of various class types in which each type differs regarding the opportunity of individual goal attainment. Nickerson (2021) notes that societal members experience a form of strain when the expectations of achieving societal goals are blocked by the legitimate means of attaining them. In some cases, as argued in Merton's classic strain theory, some individuals respond to this tension—the inability to achieve conventional goals of success—by engaging in deviant behavior (Nickerson, 2021). However, it is argued that Agnew's general strain theory develops a manifestation of deviant behavior from three primary motivators: (1) the prevention of achieving goals, (2) the removal of positive stimuli, and (3) the introduction of negative stimuli, such as the feeling of being victimized (Nivette et al., 2017).

Another aspect of strain, as it relates to the inability to achieve economic goals, can be observed through the concept of "anomie," introduced by French sociologist Emile Durkheim in 1893 (Nickerson, 2021). *Anomie* refers to a state of "normlessness," a breakdown of societal norms that influence the way people behave (Nickerson, 2021). In many cases, when people feel that they are incapable of obtaining various things (e.g., a good job, a house, a college education for their children), the assignment of blame can occur. Blame can be directed toward a variety of catalysts (e.g., government control, public policy changes, demographic shifts, etc.) that prevent people from reaching goal attainment. Those who feel like they have been wronged by others or institutions experience this feeling of normlessness, and this contributes to Durkheim's argument of anomie.

RELIGIOUS INFLUENCE

Religion plays a significant role in the lives of most people. As societies evolved from small tribes thousands of years ago to a more advanced population, people have tried to make sense of life and how they fit in this world from the macro perspective. The notion that there is a sense of accountability for the actions or behavior that were performed during a person's life plays a significant role in the decisions that people make and how they view the world. Most religious doctrines contain a common theme (i.e., the distinction of what is good and what is bad) that directs or influences the followers of that religion to abide by religious law or code. We can observe the importance of religious codes when we look back on some historical benchmark codes, such as the Ten Commandments.

When we think of how religion or the practice of a particular faith is incorporated into a person's daily life, we can observe a follower being influenced by the teachings of a spiritual leader (e.g., priest, cleric, shaman, rabbi, etc.), the lessons (in many cases through descriptive parables) garnered from the religious text, the social and psychological impact of the congregation, and the rituals that give meaning to that follower's experience. A person's religious belief in a particular doctrine can impact the way a person views the world and how they fit in it. This impact can range from a minimal influence (e.g., Jewish requirement to only eat kosher foods) all the way to a significant influence (e.g., Muslim requirement to pray five times a day).

POLITICAL INFLUENCE

As a person becomes more ingrained within society, their interpretation of how society should function or how the rule of law should be applied becomes more evident. Additionally, this is a period where people will begin to identify with a particular political party's ideology. Each party aims to achieve various ideals by passing legislation and enacting policies that, in their view, move the country in the right direction. In the United States, we have two major political parties: the Republican party and the Democratic party. As we dive deeper into this topic area, we must understand what each party stands for and how they differ.

According to the Encyclopedia Britannica (n.d.-b), the Republican party was founded in the United States 1854 and its first elected president was Abraham Lincoln. During this period, the members of the party were focused on promoting a free-market economy and pushed back on the Democratic party's direct support of using slave labor to cultivate the land, an industry supporting the economy of the Southern states. During the party's infancy, various influential political figures, such as Thomas Jefferson, were noted to favor a decentralized government with limited powers. In more recent times, the party has been aligned with dismantling many regulations that control various areas of society, such as the financial market and the environment. As Edwards (2018) explains, *conservatism* is a philosophy that posits that individual liberty is rooted in governmental systems that maintain social order.

As explained in the Encyclopedia Brittanica (n.d.-a), the other major political party (and the oldest) in the United States is the Democratic party. This party has gone through some remarkable ideological changes since it was founded in 1830 as it relates to the development of progressive public policies such as the promotion of social and economic equality in society. The Democratic party has played an instrumental role in promoting civil rights of minority groups and crafting various legislative initiatives that promote environmental protection, gun control policies, the protection of workers' rights, and the advancement of more liberal immigration laws.

A person's ideological stance on a certain societal issue can create an emotional response for some people, and the severity of that response can have a wide range. Winter (2015) argues that the application of logic and reasoning is universal in nature; however, moral sentiments and emotions are idiosyncratic. It is further argued that ideology is highly influenced by emotions and minimally based on rationality. If you think about it, we are drawn to various social issues (e.g., global warming, crime, poverty, etc.) by an emotional connection—some of which can be directly connected to some of our experiences that helped shape our belief system. When we are passionate or there is a sympathetic connection to a particular issue, our reaction to that issue is much stronger than if our connection was more empathetic in nature.

When it comes to extremism, we are observing an emotional response that is significant since the conflict that exists between that individual's ideology and the issue is significant itself. In most cases, domestic terrorist organizations and/or individuals, as with foreign terrorist organizations, will identify and unify around a particular **grievance**, an unjust activity, or some type of offense that was or has been imposed upon them. For instance, there are some people who have an extreme view on how religious beliefs should be reflected in society, and this is especially important for those who are against abortion. When the historic 1973 *Roe v. Wade* Supreme Court decision allowed for abortions to be conducted in the United States, this decision sent a shockwave through many conservative groups that are typically known to align with a right-wing ideology.

Other grievances can manifest from changes in various types of public policy that control how the United States manages domestic security issues such as illegal immigration. In many instances, right-wing political groups have attacked left-wing political groups' responses to the immigration problems at the United States' southern border. This attack has rallied those who align with a conservative or ultraconservative ideology in a manner that almost demonizes the liberal or left-wing ideological view of how border security should be managed. After President Biden initiated his 100-day halt on deportations upon taking office in 2021, we can observe far-right vigilante militia groups travelling to the border as a way of reducing the influx of migrants in areas such as Pima County, Arizona. While some people will call these groups extremist, others will argue that they are simply protecting the border and abiding by Article II of the Arizona Constitution (Fish, 2021).

When we use the term "extremism" or "extremist," we must be cautious with how these words are used or the context in which they are applied. Extremism does not necessarily mean violence; it can mean that someone's views on a particular issue are distorted or that they have such an emotional response to something that rational thinking is far removed. If we look at some of the citizen militias in the United States, while many of them are closely aligned with a right-wing extremist ideology, most of them are not violent. However, there are other cases where some of these groups are moving in a more violent direction. If we dive deeper into this topic area of right-wing and left-wing extremist ideologies, we can observe how a highly charged belief system, political party affiliation, and religious faith can all influence the emotional stability of a person or group.

Extremism manifests itself from a highly charged emotional response to a grievance or conflict with a particular issue that is impactful to the individual or group. This grievance or issue can come from the enactment of new laws, public policies, or societal changes that creates a feeling that a person's or group's standing in society has been negatively impacted or that the ability to live life as it should be lived, according to them, has been prevented. This can create an emotionally charged response. This intensity of the response can be violent in nature, or the response can lead to a more extreme way of viewing the world: a world that is misaligned with the various beliefs, political affiliations, and ideological positions important to that person or group.

SUMMARY

When we think of extremism, it is essential to view this as an irrational perspective of a local and/or world perception that has been nurtured through individual experiences and influences. Since our belief system is the foundation for determining what is important to us, a perceived threat can trigger an emotional response dedicated to protecting that belief. The type of response can be problematic since the rationale of an extremist is rooted in emotion and lacks objectivity. In many cases, the response can be both intimidating and violent.

REVIEW QUESTIONS

Directions: Based on what you have learned in this chapter, respond to the questions and prompts below.

1. What are some contributing factors that help develop a person's belief system?
2. How does an individual ideology develop?
3. How do individual grievances contribute to the development of extremist views or ideologies?

CHAPTER 3

Right-Wing and Left-Wing Extremism in the United States

GUIDING QUESTIONS

- What are the core beliefs of White extremist groups?
- How did Nazism contribute to the formation of hate groups in the United States?
- How do politics contribute to violent acts by antigovernment extremist groups?

INTRODUCTION

As mentioned previously in Chapter 1, there are two competing ideologies that exist within the United States: conservatism (right-wing) and progressivism (left-wing). The traditional philosophy of each ideology is unique, as both have a political view of how society should be managed. However, once these ideologies become extreme (i.e., a reduction in rationality and objectivity) in nature, a propensity to engage in violent behavior develops. In most cases, people who exhibit extremism or profess extreme ideologies typically fail to gain widespread acceptance and tolerance in society; this failure to gain traction or approval from the majority results in the formation of smaller groups comprised of like-minded members.

In this chapter, we will examine some of the current extremist groups that exist in the United States. It is essential that we understand the characteristics of these organizations and determine the organizational strategy for each group. As we investigate some of these featured extremist groups, there are some serious questions that have to be answered: What are the contributing factors or triggers that motivated the formation of these groups? Are these groups a fleeting formation of like-minded people, or do they have the staying power to promote their extreme ideologies? How does our government respond to their extreme ideologies?

KEY TERMS

- neo-Nazi
- Nazism
- White supremacy
- monkeywrenching

A HISTORICAL OVERVIEW OF RACE IN AMERICA

Approximately 13 million Africans and four million Native Americans were enslaved between the 16th and 19th centuries. Enslaved Africans made up roughly two thirds of the total immigrant population between the 16th and 17th centuries. Enslaved people had no laws to protect them from brutality. They were often whipped, beaten, and killed. There was no punishment for enslavers when they killed an enslaved person. The U.S. Congress outlawed the African slave trade in 1808. However, domestic trade tripled over the next 50 years. The Emancipation Proclamation freed enslaved people in 1862. However, slavery was not officially ended until the ratification of the 13th Amendment in 1865. Many people chose to disregard this amendment and sought ways to continue racial persecution. Black Codes were written to restrict the freedom of African Americans (History.com, 2021). The Ku Klux Klan (KKK) was created in 1865 and formed by a group of White supremacists who wanted to push back against Reconstruction. They were an extremely violent group and killed many. Congress suppressed the KKK in 1882; however, they reemerged in the 1920s, 1960s, and, most recently, in the modern day (Aron, 2018). The KKK have been joined in their reign of **White supremacy** by groups such as the Proud Boys, the Boogaloo movement, the Aryan Nations, and many others. The Proud Boys are the figureheads of modern-day White

FIGURE 3.1 Ku Klux Klan March, 1927

supremacy. To further understand how these right-wing groups have evolved in the United States, we will explore how foreign influences and domestic grievances intersect to form this particular ideology.

THE RIGHT-WING EXTREMIST THREAT

RACIST, ANTIGOVERNMENT, AND HATE GROUPS

When we hear the term "neo-Nazi," a variety of images can manifest in our minds. We could invoke such imagery as the swastika, Adolf Hitler, shaved heads, and concentration camps. Members of **neo-Nazi** groups are infatuated with Hitler and his ambition to conquer the world through his once-powerful Third Reich. This government or regime was focused on creating a world through **Nazism** that consisted of an Aryan race, or superior race. However, as noted by the Holocaust Encyclopedia (2020), "The term *Aryan* was originally used to identify the Indo-European or Indo-Germanic peoples who settled through India, Persia, and Europe thousands of years earlier." European scholars initially used this term to describe the similarities between European, Sanskrit, and Persian languages; however, the term was later misapplied to describe an ethnicity or race (Holocaust Encyclopedia, 2020).

During this period, between 1919 and 1945, the Nazi party (also known as the National Socialist German Workers' party) evolved through a variety of political maneuvering and, in some cases, through violent activities (Encyclopedia Britannica, n.d.-c). The Nazi party used Germany's Great Depression of 1929 as a way of justifying the need for the party to save the country. This National Socialist movement was born out of the negative social and economic impact that had manifested post–World War I and the German people feeling demoralized from a particularly bleak outlook on their individual lives. In circumstances such as these, people often look for someone to blame. Unfortunately, the Jewish population was targeted as being the main contributor to Germany's problems. The Jewish people and the past mishandling of German politics (as it relates to the consequences of the Treaty of Versailles) became the focal points (or scapegoats) Hitler used to justify a dramatic change in German politics. The Nazi party focused on systematically controlling the political influences that governed Germany, including various social and cultural activities of the German people. Essentially, Hitler was able to gain the support of the German police, intelligence, and military through a couple of power moves to gain authority; for example, when the German president Paul von Hindenburg died, Hitler positioned himself to take the presidency (Encyclopedia Britannica, n.d.-c).

As World War II began in the European theater, it was later discovered that Hitler's regime began to round up those of the Jewish faith, placed them in concentration camps, and operationalized his famous *Final Solution*: a method to exterminate those who did not fit the mold of the so-called Aryan race. These mass murders were carried out at a variety of concentration camps throughout Germany and Poland. The extermination camps that

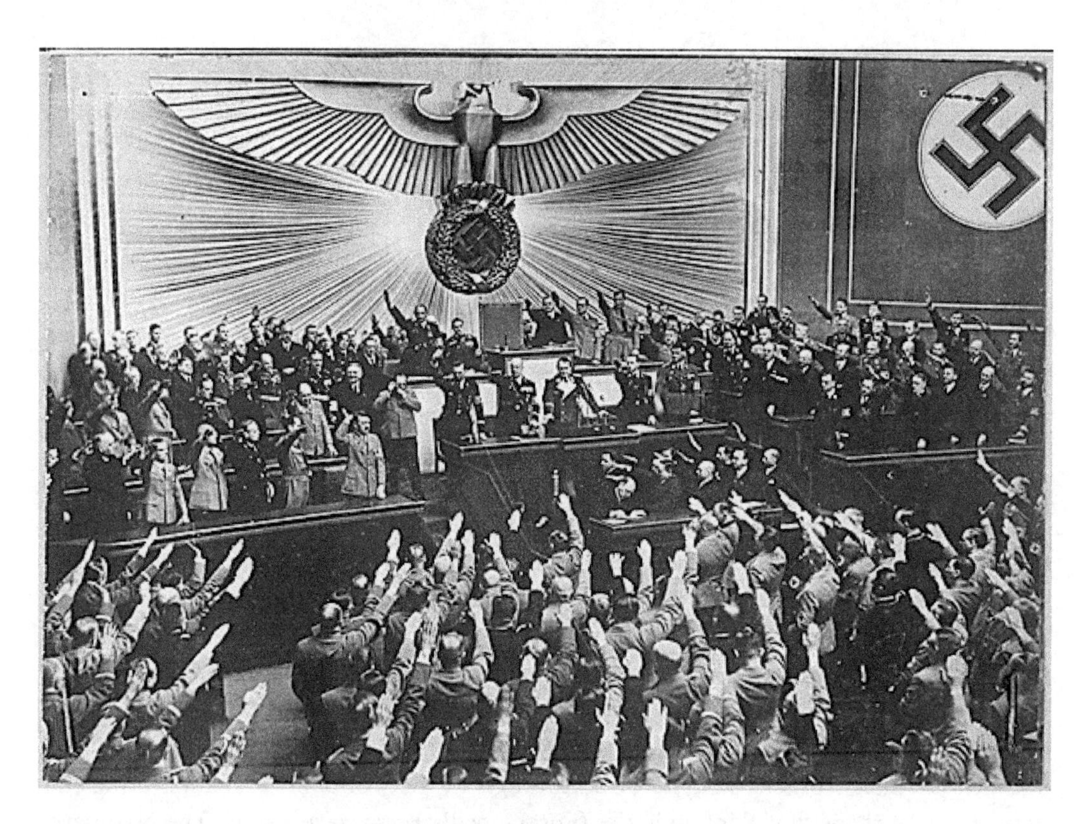

FIGURE 3.2 Hitler Accepts the Ovation of the Reichstag, 1938

became the most famous, based on their ability to conduct mass murder through gas chambers and the incineration of the remains through large crematories, can be seen at Auschwitz, Majdanek, and Treblinka (Encyclopedia Britannica, n.d.-d). Those who remain aligned with a racist (antisemitic) ideology that welcomes or promotes violence as a way of protecting that ideology use the atrocities that were committed by the Third Reich as a motivator for their behavior. They use the writings of Hitler, such as *Mein Kampf* (or my struggle), as their doctrine, which contributes to the legitimacy of their ideology and provides a justification that their way of thinking is not isolated to a small segment of the population. With respect to a more domestically produced doctrine that was created by a United States citizen, *The Turner Diaries*, authored by William Pierce, has also been used as a reference point for right-wing extremists who promote White supremacy. To further understand how impactful the Nazi party was and continues to be, we will examine some of the right-wing extremist groups in the United States.

The Right-Wing Extremist Conspiracy

While *Mein Kampf* has been used to support various recruitment efforts and ideological arguments for right-wing extremist groups, the so-called "replacement theory" or the "great replacement" conspiracy has become a focal point for justifying a xenophobic position for white citizens (Jones, 2022). The origin of the great replacement can be observed in the writings of authors such as Renaud Camus and Charles Pearson (Wilson & Flanagan, 2022). Essentially, this theory explains that the White population will soon become the minority while the non-White population will become the majority (Wilson & Flanagan, 2022). For a person that maintains a racist ideology, the notion of becoming inferior to minority groups creates a severe level of consternation. In some cases, we can observe this theory or conspiracy as supporting the justification of violence towards minority groups.

An example of how replacement theory has impacted or influenced a person to commit a violent act can be observed in the mass shooting event that occurred at the Tops Friendly Markets store in Buffalo, New York, on May 14, 2022 (Freile & Lahman, 2022). The suspected shooter was a white 18-year-old who selected a geographic location that was heavily populated with Black community members; he is suspected of killing ten customers who were purchasing groceries in the store with an AR-15 style rifle (Freile & Lahman, 2022). Law enforcement officials have communicated that the suspected shooter had posted a 180-page manifesto rooted in racist ramblings that justified his intention of committing violence against another race (Crane & Fonrouge, 2022). Indeed, Samuel R. Delany was absolutely correct when he said, "Words mean things." The questionable thematic rhetoric that insinuates a growing threat of societal diversity touted in the media, the toxic Internet chat rooms that contribute to the process of radicalization, and the divisive language used by our political leaders all contribute to the perpetuation of the great replacement paranoia.

National Alliance (NA)

As explained by the Southern Poverty Law Center (SPLC, n.d.-c),the National Alliance (NA) was formed in 1970 in Mill Point, West Virginia. The organization was founded by William Pierce, who once held a physics professor position at Oregon State University from 1962 to 1965. This right-wing extremist group is aligned with White supremacy and has promoted violence for all non-White races (primarily Jews) so that the United States becomes an all-White nation. The ideology of NA is explained in the following quote by the organization (as cited in SPLC, n.d.-c):

> Our world is hierarchical. Each of us is a member of the Aryan (or "European") race, which, like the other races, developed its special characteristics over many thousands of years. ... Those races which evolved in the more demanding environment of the North, where surviving a winter required planning and self-discipline, advance more rapidly in the development of the higher mental faculties than those which remained in the unvarying climate of the tropics. (In Its Own Words section)

Based on this statement, we can observe that this group is philosophically aligned with how the Nazi party viewed the world. The characteristics associated with this shared philosophy/ideology are closely related to Darwin's theory of evolution (or Darwinism), which promoted the idea that certain species survive (from a biological perspective) by natural selection, meaning there are circumstances that allow a species to exist or evolve because they adapt to an ever-changing environment (Encyclopedia Britannica, n.d.-e).

By utilizing some of the arguments found in Darwinsim (as interpreted and used to fit their philosophical narrative) and coupling the scientific principles from that theory with a racist/extremist ideology, this organization can promote its beliefs and gain membership for its organization. Pierce was a savvy business professional throughout his time at the National Alliance. To support the organization's sustainability, Pierce purchased a White-power music label that contributed to National Alliance's revenue stream. Additional sources of revenue came from the sale of books, cassettes, and racist paraphernalia (SPLC, n.d.-c). The National Alliance has a history of various members engaging in violent crimes, such as bank robberies, police shootouts, and a failed bombing attempt at the main approach to Disney World in Florida (SPLC, n.d.-c).

Just before Pierce's death in 2002, the National Alliance was earning over $1 million a year, and the organization had a regular broadcast of racist/hate rhetoric that kept the business model sustainable (SPLC, n.d.-c). However, the viability and continuation of the organization shifted toward a downhill trajectory when the new organizational leader, Erich Gliebe, assumed control. Essentially, Gliebe made a variety of decisions and some controversial comments that alienated other hate groups, which led to a significant loss of organizational members (SPLC, n.d.-c). More recently, in 2018, Will Williams II, who assumed a top leadership role in the National Alliance, was convicted of misdemeanor battery on one of his former employees who worked in the organization as a clerk (Barrouquere, 2018). Ultimately, the organization has largely been a failure; however, while the organization has lost its standing within the neo-Nazi community, the ideology has lived on in other hate groups.

Creativity Movement

The Creativity Movement is a White supremacist organization that was originally formed in 1973 by Ben Klassen (a former Florida state legislator) under the name the Church of the Creator (Anti-Defamation League, n.d.-a). Klassen committed suicide in 1993, and Matt Hale took over the organization's leadership position, and the group was later named the Creativity Movement (Michael, 2006). It maintains a strict neo-Nazi ideology that leans on religious rhetoric to help support their credibility and appeal to other potential members who not only align their political beliefs with having a society dominated by White people but also feel a spiritual responsibility for fulfilling the demands of a worldwide revolution or racial holy war. The ideology of the Creativity Movement is explained in the following quote by the organization (as cited in SPLC, n.d.-b):

> We gird for total war against the Jews and the rest of the goddamned mud races of the world—politically, militantly, financially, morally, and religiously. We regard it as the heart of our religious creed and as the most sacred credo of all. We regard it as a holy war to the finish—a racial holy war. Rahowa! Is INEVITABLE. ... No longer can the mud races and the White Race live on the same planet. (In Its Own Words section)

This group is highly influenced by the same ideology that drove the Nazis to behave as they did under Hitler; however, Klassen wrote a variety of texts that helped define the purpose of the White race. Various books, such as *Nature's Eternal Religion*, *Rahowa!*, *This Planet Is All Ours*, and *The White Man's Bible,* help support the overarching doctrine that guides the organization's mission (SPLC, n.d.-b). As listed in the book's title, *Rahowa* is an abbreviated term for "racial holy war," which is the group's call to violence.

This group is known to have members who have committed racially targeted murder and the bombings of churches and other nonprofit organizations. For instance, George Loeb, a leader of the Church of the Creator, was arrested and charged with shooting Harold Mansfield, a Black sailor and Persian Gulf War veteran who served on the *U.S.S. Saratoga* in the U.S. Navy (Word, 1992). The shooting occurred after a near collision of vehicles in a parking lot (Word, 1992). Another set of arrests occurred when eight suspected White supremacists of the organization were accused of breaking firearms laws, and another member was accused of plotting the assassination of Rodney G. King (Newton & O'Neill, 1993). Finally, the leader of the organization, Matt Hale, was arrested and convicted of soliciting someone to kill a federal judge who was presiding over the copyright case that dealt with the organization's former name, the World Church of the Creator (Wilgoren, 2003).

Aryan Nations (AN)

The Aryan Nations (AN), originally named the Church of Jesus Christ Christian, Aryan Nations, was founded in the 1970s by Richard Girnt Butler (Barkun, 1990). Butler began to further develop his racist neo-Nazi ideology in the 1960s while he was employed as an aeronautical engineer at Lockheed in Southern California (Balch, 2006, p. 85). He was heavily influenced by Dr. Wesley Swift, the founder of the Church of Jesus Christ Christian, and William Potter Gale, a retired U.S. Army colonel who served in World War II and was on the staff of General Douglas MacArthur (Balch, 2006, p. 85; SLPC, n.d.-a). After Swift's death, Butler formed his own organization, based on the religious doctrine of Swift's teachings, and named it the Aryan Nations—a political arm of the Church of Jesus Christ Christian.

According to Balch (2006), Butler believed that Jesus Christ was not a Jew and that White people, during this period, were the descendants of the Lost Tribes of Israel. Moreover, Butler also believed that Jewish people were the children of Satan who were bound to dominate the world and make White Christian civilizations subservient. While many followers of the Identity Movement have debated the origin of the Jewish population, the "seedline" doctrine was widely embraced by Butler, and this contributed to the organization's ideology (Balch, 2006, p. 85). The *seedline doctrine* posits that Jews are the offspring of the Christian biblical figure Eve and Satan (Balch, 2006, p. 86).

The Aryan Nations was formed in Idaho, and the organization was positioned in a compound in the rural area of Coeur d'Alene. The goal of this organization was to unify all those other groups and individuals who maintain the same ideological and racist view of the society in which they live. Butler implemented various strategies to unify the racist leaders around the world by holding an annual Aryan World Congress on the compound. There was also an Aryan Youth Assembly (a congregation of young followers that is reminiscent of the Hitler youth from World War II) held at the compound in April every year.

The Aryan Nations has spawned a variety of violent extremist members who engaged in various criminal and even terroristic activities that garnered national attention. The organization was essentially reduced to a shell of its former self when an Idaho jury awarded $6.3 million to a family that was chased, shot at, and assaulted by AN security guards when the family drove too close to the compound's property line (Balch, 2006, p. 81). Between the organization's financial woes, internal conflict, loss of members, and continued pressure exerted by law enforcement, the organization had disintegrated into ashes upon Butler's death in 2004.

The Order

The Order, an American White supremacist group, was founded by Robert Jay Mathews in the 1980s. Mathews, as a child, joined the right-wing John Birch Society and the Mormon Church (McClary, 2006). Later in life, Mathews formed an anticommunist militia group, the Sons of Liberty, that was made up of survivalists and other members who were aligned with the Mormon faith (McClary, 2006). As Mathews became more extreme in his ideology, he focused his efforts on the development of a more violent White supremacist group. While Mathews preferred to call the new organization Bruder Schwigen (Silent Brotherhood), various members remained adamant about calling the group The Order since it was similar to the fictionalized organization, called by the same name, in the William Pierce book *The Turner Diaries*. Mathews was a regular member of the Aryan Nations and the National Alliance. The Order was aligned with the neo-Nazi ideology and promoted the philosophy of the racist Christian Identity movement (Encyclopedia Britannica, n.d.-f).

Since members of The Order have followed the philosophy of the Christian Identity movement, this quasireligious belief supported the rationality behind the group's behavior. As with other extremist groups, the ideology of that organization is only as strong as the belief system of its members and the unique doctrine or philosophy that provides the justification for their behavior. For example, as a way of obtaining financial resources to support the organization, members from The Order would attack pimps, drug dealers, and other people who were behaving in a way that they thought was against God's will (Encyclopedia Britannica, n.d.-f). In many instances, The Order distinguished itself as a more violent White supremacist group that supported criminal activity, including participating in events that can be classified as domestic terrorism.

The Order has been involved in various high-profile crimes that garnered national attention. For example, in 1985, ten members of the organization were convicted of racketeering and other criminal charges that identified their overall goal of financing a civil war against the federal government (Associated Press, 1985). During the trial, the prosecution witnesses testified that members of The Order were planning to assassinate prominent Jews and television network presidents who were considered to be enemies of the Christian Identity and God (Associated Press, 1985). Another very high-profile crime occurred when Alan Berg, who was a radio talk show host in Denver, was killed in an assassination-style murder outside of his residence on June 19, 1984 (Malcolm, 1984). Berg was noted to be a controversial figure who would provoke critical responses to various comments made by the listening audience. Additional crimes involved armored truck robberies, counterfeiting money, and the bombing of a synagogue in Boise, Idaho (Elfrink, 2018). One armored truck robbery, which involved a Brink's truck, ended with The Order members stealing $3.6 million (Elfrink, 2018). However, The Order's reign of terror was quickly coming to an end at the later portion of 1984.

The FBI was actively involved in trying to locate Mathews for his role in various crimes connected to the organization. On December 8, 1984, Mathews's whereabouts were reported to the FBI as being a cabin at Whidbey Island in Seattle, Washington. Approximately 150 FBI agents surrounded the cabin, and a 35-hour standoff ensued (Elfrink, 2018). At some point, the FBI had fired flares into the cabin, causing it to catch on fire; simultaneously, Mathews fired his submachine gun back at the agent (Elfrink, 2018). In the end, Mathews succumbed to the flames, and his body was later recovered inside the cabin (Elfrink, 2018). After the death of Mathews, the FBI continued to charge additional members of The Order for other crimes, such as racketeering (Jimison, 2018).

Aryan Brotherhood

As the weight of social acknowledgment has turned into the standard in numerous communities, groups have developed quickly. Numerous gangs throughout communities are characterized as being criminal groups. The National Institute of Justice defines a *gang* as individuals who relate to a group, which creates an air of terrorizing with illegal plans and targets. As communities are associated with the formation of gangs, many of the gang's affiliated members end up captured, indicted, and jailed. At last, all the gangs in the community stretch into the restorative framework. Prison gangs are otherwise called security risk groups. The prison gangs are looked to be more dangerous and violent than the gangs within community settings. Usually, prison gangs carry on with criminal action while detained and still have huge authority over street gangs. As per the research led by the National Gang Intelligence Center, many prison gangs are slippery on account of their isolation from general society and their capacity to be unnoticed in detainment facilities, which enables brutal acts to be submitted that in the end influence all dimensions of law authorization (Hamm, 2018).

While there are a critical number of prison gangs across the country, a few groups have a more significant number of associated individuals. In the late 1960s, California experienced acts by a gang group named Aryan Brotherhood (AB). The Aryan Brotherhood was composed of a huge number of individuals across the nation, both imprisoned and in the community. While the Aryan Brotherhood is just one of numerous prison gangs, remedial overseers are continually faced with prison gangs' opponents and posse-related acts. Remedial executives should address the issue by distinguishing crucial data, for example, the historical backdrop of the group and all the gang rivalry. This will permit correctional administrators the ability to implement strategies to possibly maintain distance from prison gang brutality

Structure and History of the Aryan Brotherhood

The existence of the Aryan Brotherhood in California San Quentin prison is rooted in the year 1967. From 1950 to 1960, the gang was initially named the Blue Bird Gang. The name was changed because the group understood that to develop in numbers and shield themselves from the more prominent Black and Hispanic gangs, more members were required. Therefore, in 1976, the evolution of the Aryan Brotherhood started. Their motto "one is in forever; the main way out is dead" shows that any individuals who joined the gang would portray the group for the remainder of their lives. At first, the group enabled only White, partially Irish individuals to join. Later, the group turned into a racial domination gang. The Aryan Brotherhood might be unidentifiable to correctional administrators at first; however, the gang has symbolic tattoos that are recognizable to other associates.

The Aryan Brotherhood members distinguish themselves with tattoos, including AB initials, the swastika, 666, double lightning bolts, and clovers. The clover was embraced from its Irish foundation. The triple six tattoo speaks to the sign of the brute. Regularly, the individuals who distinguished themselves utilizing the 666 had the numbers inside a shamrock. Also, the swastika signifies "one is unique," which is another indicator of a gang member.

Alongside identifying member tattoos, the Aryan Brotherhood has significant stipulations and gang guidance. The mission statement for the Aryan Brotherhood was "I will remain by my sibling, my sibling will precede all others, my life is relinquished should I fall flat my sibling, I will respect my sibling in harmony and war" (Pratte, 2016). While the gangs at first framed the group to conflict with Hispanic and Black people, throughout the years, the Aryan Brotherhood made a working association with the

Mexican Mafia (Rafael, 2007). Even though the connection between the two gang groups is a matter of fact, the Aryan Brotherhood has since contradicted the contention of the Mexican Mafia la Nuestra Familia. Likewise, the Aryan Brotherhood has enthusiastic scorn for Black gangs, which is why their adversaries are the Bloods, Crips, Black Guerilla Family, and the El Rukns (Florida Department of Corrections, n.d.). While the group has changed specific criteria since it came into existence, the Aryan Brotherhood has a broad history of violations submitted in the California Department of Corrections.

Between 1975 and 1985, more than 40 homicides and 26 murders were committed by Aryan Brotherhood members in California jails and prisons (Fong et al., 2013). Between 1978 and 1992, three of the casualties were the correctional staff (Fong et al., 2013). Moreover, the Aryan Brotherhood is known for administering illegal imports throughout the jails (e.g., cellphones and drugs), typically aided by their female partners. The Aryan Brotherhood contains an exceptionally unnoticeable enrollment, making this gang group significantly more savage since they are not effectively recognizable. The gang has leaders who have been in the California Corrections since the late 1970s. At present, the legislature is trying to tie a significant number of the in-house jail murders to famous leaders of the Aryan Brotherhood. The Aryan Brotherhood still holds substantial sovereignty throughout the California Department of Corrections.

Currently, a portion of those accepted to be subsidiary with the Aryan Brotherhood has been in isolation for more than a quarter of a century. The inmates chose to begin a hunger strike throughout the prisons, which included an expected 20,500 out of California's 115,000 detainees (Pelz et al., 2016). This hunger strike was intended to end single isolations lengths but also outlines how effective the Aryan Brotherhood is inside the prisons. Since the hunger strike, the California Department of Corrections has been moving known gang leaders and individuals from isolation into the general population.

GANG VIOLENCE IN PRISONS

The California Department of Corrections has determined that confining gang individuals from an all-inclusive community is an issue that should be amended. According to the present research, about 3,000 detainees are being held in isolation throughout the California Corrections—all members of the dynamic gang. The Undersecretary of Operations Terri McDonald, as part of the California Corrections, has expressed that the office implemented the arrangement of isolation in an endeavor to warrant institutional and open security. The California Department of Corrections thought something must be done to counteract demonstrations of jail gang brutality. As indicated by the documentation of the policies and plans for security threat groups, the detainee must earn the right to join the general population by demonstrating to the staff they will not practice unacceptable behavior in the community.

The California Department of Corrections has laid out three measures to protect against groups that bring insecurity among people and violence resulting from gang attacks. Firstly, partnered-group individuals are given the Advisement of Expectations Diagram amid prisoner intake. Also, a video for security danger assembles redirection, notwithstanding the material referencing the detainment facility's resistance for posse-related exercises. Finally, the California Department of Corrections has programs to deal with groups that pose a danger or insecurity. Program activities to forestall group viciousness include Substituting Projects for Fierceness, Intelligent to Transformation, Revolution Companies Journaling Sequences, Seven Conducts on the Inside, Gangs Unidentified, and Defiance Barriers. Likewise, these projects will be offered to guilty parties in isolation who need to go into the all-inclusive community. For prisoners who never again wish to have any group association, the California Department of Corrections offers the Step Down Program to help detainees progress. While this is a beginning to safety, other state remedial offices execute a more specific technique for prison gang initiatives.

While the State of California has attempted to forestall jail group brutality, the ongoing arrival of detainees in isolation that are being exchanged to the all-inclusive community has lessened altogether. This strategy has all the earmarks of being a noteworthy advance for the California Department of Corrections; however, it is insufficient. In the ongoing years, the office implemented this arrangement because of a detainee hunger strike. The craving strike originated from prisoners in isolation, exclusively as a result of their group connection. In 2012, the California Department of Corrections had 3,923 detainees in security housing units and 7,007 in administrative segregation units (Richardson, 2015). Currently, the office has 2,211 detainees in the security housing unit and 2,643 prisoners in the administrative segregation unit (Richardson, 2015). Now, the office concentrates more on lodging detainees in isolation dependent on social issues rather than posse association. In fact, the numbers have diminished severely; however, viable projects and protection measures are still not implemented. Numerous jail posse counteractive strategies incorporate concealment, social intercession, network association projects, and arrangement of chances.

The California Department of Corrections made steps to lessen the quantity of singularly restricted detainees, yet little effort to keep group action from occurring once the prisoners are discharged into the all-inclusive community. Groups are tricky in the case of thinking about network well-being or social request inside the jails. Furthermore, according to Provost (2017), remedial overseers must determine what security danger represents a more significant risk for propagating jail viciousness. In 1970, California experienced gigantic social programming slices that added to the ascent of packs. Also, the 1978 California Proposition 13 included cutting various socially subsidized programs. Mulling over all data, remedial department heads ought to be aware of security risk bunch programming and the general effect that group programming will have on prisoners.

Gang Renouncement and Disassociation (GRAD) is a program of the Texas Department of Corrections, which was started by the Texas Security Threat Group Management Office.

A detainee must meet specific criteria to participate in the program. The requirements include the following (Texas Prisoners Network Support, n.d.; Fleisher, 2017):

- no offender or staff assaults for at least 2 years;
- no major disciplinary cases for at least 1 year;
- no extortion cases for at least 2 years;
- no weapon possession cases for at least 2 years;
- no aggressive sexual misconduct cases for at least 2 years;
- must have level one status for a minimum of 1 year;
- must have renounced membership in a security threat group; and
- must not have been involved in any security threat group act for a minimum of 2 years

When detainees are acknowledged into the program, the group member disassociation is separated into three stages: Stage one incorporates substance misuse classes, AA, and chaplaincy recordings for two months. Stage two includes a scholarly contribution, the executives, and addictive criminal conduct. The last stage incorporates an educational module of a half-day work plan. This program is exclusive with the end goal of pack individuals leaving the group they are with and joining the all-inclusive community and being appointed to a unit prescribed by the state classification committee.

The Washington State Department of Corrections led an investigation to find accepted procedures for managing groups that are a threat to security. Amid the study, the division recognized the need to update intercultural guidance for pack individuals to learn positive viewpoints about their race and ethnicity. Likewise, according to Joyce (2016), more staff is expected to concentrate exclusively on security risk aggregate insight and ban. The directors included suggestions that could upgrade the general effort, for example, actualizing strategies to encourage prisoner lodging dependent on progression in the program, distinguishing and creating instruments to proficiently archive wrongdoing from an outside source, advancing higher learning, and examining pack-related exercises per unit. Moreover, the division chairpersons included tattoo expulsion and mediation from nearby specialists and experts, and projects executives to distinguish and create frameworks to record, measure, and examine security danger as individuals advance. The endeavors made by the Washington State Department of Corrections Administrators are critical steps in the push to avert posse viciousness and groups that are a threat to security.

Migrating detainees to the general populace is just the initial step; numerous means ought to be pursued to guarantee effective procedure. In Texas and Washington, the group-related activity centers around detainees gaining direct access into the entire community with projects geared toward individuals recording part disassociation. Washington State goes above and beyond by giving access to classes that show individuals their social foundation and allowing prisoners the chance to expel tattoos with pack images. The California Department of Corrections has made the underlying advance of moving detainees to the all-inclusive community, yet more programming should be utilized. Maybe the strategies of the Washington Department of Corrections can help the California Department of Corrections to implement endeavors to avoid pack brutality. Numerous restorative staff state that while it is difficult to successfully implement projects that dispel jail groups, programs can be set up to prevent posse exercises and brutality in any event.

THE PROUD BOYS

To say the least, the Proud Boys are an interesting organization. Gavin McInnes, a far-right commentator, founded the Proud Boys in New York City in 2016 (Kriner & Lewis, 2021). McInnes was born in England in 1970 and immigrated to Ontario; he resides in the United States as a legal immigrant from Canada (Gollner, 2021). According to Arkin (2021), the Proud Boys has been identified as a hate group. The Anti-Defamation League further supports this designation, as it characterizes the organization as violent, nationalistic, Islamaphobic, transphobic, and misogynist (Arkin, 2021). The Canadian government has designated the Proud Boys as a terrorist entity (Gollner, 2021).

Interestingly, the Proud Boys are comprised of other minority groups; also noteworthy, their current chairman, Henry "Enrique" Tarrio, is of Latino ethnicity (Arkin, 2021). The organization has more than 40 chapters across the country and total membership of just under 40,000; each chapter operates semiautonomously (Yousef, 2021). Members of this organization have been known to engage in street fights against Antifa activists and other violent actions committed against members of the Black Lives Matter (BLM) group (Yousef, 2021). The FBI. has categorized the Proud Boys as an extremist group with ties to White nationalism (Wilson, 2018). In 2018, Gavin McInnes renounced his affiliation with the group; however, he argued against the racist designation of the group and accused the media of spreading the "great White supremacy hoax" (Oroszi & Ellis, 2019).

Another unique aspect of this group involves their participation with "Stop the Steal," referring to the idea that the presidency was "stolen" from Donald Trump in the 2020 election. While the Proud Boys had little national recognition since their formation, this status changed when former president Donald Trump was asked to denounce far-right groups, similar to the Proud Boys; his response was to "stand back and stand by" (Yousef, 2021). In some ways, this comment lent credence to the Proud Boys, and this acknowledgment further emboldened the group to support the president. Based on the past rhetoric that had come from Trump, the Proud Boys and other far-right groups could have seen an intersection of ideological positions on certain societal issues.

The Proud Boys continued their support of Trump when they arrived to Washington, DC, on January 6, 2021, to be participants in the "Stop the Steal" rally (Kriner & Lewis, 2021). While many people have argued that insurrection was a form of protest that evolved and was not planned, they fail to observe the setting or characteristics of what developed from the rally. While the group describes themselves on their website (as cited by Kriner & Lewis, 2021) as being Western chauvinists who are a libertarian-oriented fraternal drinking club, they came to the rally wearing ballistic vests; members were wearing a quasiuniform set that had presented the group's insignia and organizational colors. They were also utilizing encrypted communications equipment to coordinate movements from the rally to the Capitol. It was later found that a key member of the Oath Keepers had coordinated the movement toward and on the Capitol with the Proud Boys; their mutual goal was stopping the certification of the presidential vote (Lokay, Robinson, & Crenshaw, 2021).

THE OATH KEEPERS

The SPLC (n.d.-d) explains that the Oath Keepers were founded in 2009 by a former U.S. Army paratrooper Elmer "Stewart" Rhodes in Nevada. The organization has been designated as an antigovernment extremist group, and it focuses on the recruitment of both police and military veterans. Having an antigovernment organization that is comprised of former or active members is an interesting characteristic of the group since both the police and military are enforcement arms of the United States government. The Oath Keepers believe in upholding the U.S. Constitution; however, their interpretation of the document diverges from that of lawmakers and judges.

There have been many instances where the Oath Keepers travelled to various areas of the United States experiencing some form of civil unrest. They arrive at these locations to interrupt or interfere with how law enforcement or other government organizations respond. For example, in 2015, Oath Keepers had responded to support Rick Barclay and George Backes, two gold miners, by being a security element to prevent a possible threat of BLM members attacking Barclay and Backes's property. The Oath Keepers also went Ferguson, Missouri, in response to the protests that erupted over the shooting of Michael Brown in 2015 (Fowler, 2015). Members of the groups would stand watch over businesses and apartments, armed with rifles, and much of their efforts were supported by business owners. However, the group gained a new level of notoriety as they descended on Washington, DC, on January 6, 2021.

In 2022, Rhodes and 10 other members of the Oath Keepers were charged with seditious conspiracy due to their participatory activities during the January 6, 2021, U.S. Capitol insurrection (Kelly, 2022). Rhodes had a variety of communications (text messages and other various chats) that articulated that the riot's goal was to intimidate Congress by establishing groups of people to engage in various tactics to gain entry into the Capitol Building. Text messages from other group members discussed the use and distribution of weapons, including training that would support the riot's success (Balsamo et al., 2022). The indictment also describes that various Oath Keeper teams were positioned to confront Capitol police officers and were equipped with firearms to stop the lawful transfer of power (Balsamo et al., 2022).

TRUMP'S ERA OF WHITE SUPREMACY

Donald Trump's bid for the presidency in 2016 led to a new wave of White supremacists. Suddenly, they had a figurehead who believed in their rhetoric. Former President Trump was known to utter, "Laziness is a trait in blacks"; "They're rapists" in reference to Mexican immigrants (Phillips, 2017); and "Grab 'em by the pussy. You can do anything" (Trautman, 2017). Trump called for a total ban on Muslims entering the United States. During a campaign rally, Trump saw a White man assault a Black man and went on to offer legal assistance to the White man. Trump's campaign slogan "Make America Great Again" resonated with White people living in poverty. White men and women flocked to him. They firmly and forcefully believed that he would sweep them into a new world. Essentially, the Proud Boys evolved from a simple street gang into an international organization. They currently have chapters all over the United States and in Canada, the United Kingdom, and in other continents (Dimson, Marsh, & Staunton, 2009).

Trump won the presidential seat over Hillary Clinton in 2016. This victory seemed to legitimize White supremacist views. Trump continued with his racist views during his presidency. For example, he attacked NFL players who kneeled during the national anthem (Frederick, Pegoraro, & Schmidt, 2020). He said, "Wouldn't you love to see one of these NFL owners, when somebody disrespects our flag, to say, 'Get that son of a bitch off the field right now. Out! He's fired.'" (Boykoff, 2021). Trump continued with his outright support of White supremacists, which led to many terrorist attacks during his presidency. Right-wing extremists made up two thirds of attacks and plots within the United States during 2019. January 1, 2020, to May 8, 2020, saw that number rise to 90% (Jones, 2020). In 2017, a neo-Nazi drove his car into antiracist protestors in Virginia (Packer, 2022). In 2018, a White supremacist conducted a mass shooting at a Pittsburgh, PA, synagogue (Leander et al., 2020). These are just a few examples of the many attacks conducted by White supremacists during Trump's presidency.

THE CAPITOL RIOT

The "Save America" rally held on January 6, 2021, quickly turned into a riot. Former President Trump started the rally at 11 a.m., telling the gathered crowd that the election was stolen. At 1:10 p.m., Trump ended his speech and urged the gathered crowd to take back their country forcefully and walk on the Capitol. Trump's followers answered his call for violence and started breaching the Capitol before the rally was over. At 1:26 p.m. Capitol police ordered the evacuation of the Library of Congress. At 2:11 p.m., rioters breached police lines. They would go on to scale the walls and enter the Capitol Building. By 2:47, the rioters had broken into the Chamber of Congress. The first reported fatality occurred at 3:34 p.m. (an Air Force veteran rioter). At 8:00 p.m. Congress reconvened. Five people were killed, and many others were injured. Also, many Capitol police officers have since taken their lives (Hawkins & Simon-Roberts, 2022).

FIGURE 3.3 Trump Supporters Gathered at the West Entrance of the U.S. Capitol

An estimated 800 followers stormed the Capitol that day. The Proud Boys were told by Trump "to stand by." The rioters were primarily White males around 34 years old (Jordan & Dykes, 2022). Among them were Proud Boys, Boogaloo members, and other far-right members. However, a majority of the rioters were regular Trump followers and were not known affiliates of any White supremacist group. There is evidence that the Capitol Riot was planned well in advance. Most of the planning happened online between people all over the United States. Proud Boys and Boogaloo members were told not to wear their usual clothing. They were to blend in with the riot and be incognito (Benda, 2021). This attack is perhaps the most notorious during former President Trump's time in office.

THE LEFT-WING EXTREMIST THREAT

As we have previously discussed, right-wing extremist organizations (and individual actors) maintain an ideology that is primarily concerned with racial or ethnic supremacy, an opposition to government at the local, state, and federal levels, and the fight against certain public policies (e.g., Roe v. Wade; abortion rights) that go against their beliefs (Jones

& Doxsee, 2020). However, if we examine the left-wing extremist organizations' ideology, we can observe some marked differences with the right-wing ideology. Left-wing extremist organizations are focused on maintaining various oppositional strategies against capitalism, imperialism, and colonialism; to include the protection of the United States' natural environment (Jones & Doxsee, 2020). While there have been left-wing extremist threats and attacks in the United States over the past 50 years, the violence of these groups and individual actors are far less frequent than those who align with right-wing extremism. However, there has been a formation of new left-wing groups or revolutionary organizations in the United States that have had their ideological positions questioned as they have responded to various events that lead to violent outcomes.

One particular left-wing group and or ongoing revolutionary movement that has become more popular over that past 5 years, has been called "Antifa" which is shortened from the term "anti-fascist." This loosely organized group was formed in 2017 in response to a white supremacist Unite the Right rally in Charlottesville, Virginia (Anti-Defamation League, n.d.-b). As noted by the Anti-Defamation League (n.d.-b), Antifa is characterized as being a decentralized and leaderless group that is opposed to fascism in the United States. Fascism, a popular ideology of the 20th century in Europe, has been incorporated into political strategies that would blame that country's economic issues on individuals or groups that were categorized as minorities (Encyclopedia Britannica, n.d.-g). As observed in Germany and Italy (led by Prime Minister Benito Mussolini) in the early to mid-1940s, the fascism ideology fostered each country's move towards extreme nationalism, militarism, and racial purity (Encyclopedia Britannica, n.d.-g). Many of the tactics used by Antifa members have included vandalism, looting, physical altercations with others, and harassment (Anti-Defamation League, n.d.-b; Jones, 2020). According to the Anti-Defamation League (n.d.-b), there has been one antifa-related murder that occurred in 2020 in Portland, Oregon.

Another group or movement that has gained popularity since the shooting death of Trayvon Martin in 2013 and the 2014 death of Eric Garner is Black Lives Matter (BLM) (Anti-Defamation League, n.d.-c). The BLM movement started with the use of their hashtag (#BlackLivesMatter) and has evolved to the formation of a physical group presence that occupies areas for the purpose of demonstrations (Anti-Defamation League, n.d.-c). Like Antifa, BLM is a decentralized organization that is coordinated by local leaders who seek support from the group so that specific grievances can be aired publicly (Anti-Defamation League, n.d.-c). While BLM has been primarily aligned with being a social movement that is dedicated towards changes in public policy that support minority groups, there have been instances where the violence and destruction have overshadowed their primary cause (Anti-Defamation League, n.d.-c). Efforts have been made by BLM leadership to combat disinformation that has been published on the Internet. There have been a variety of online posts that have illustrated the group as being anti-white, associated with vandalism of local businesses, and a hate group;

however, it has been proven that many of these accusations are promoted by opposing groups (right-wing extremist and non-extremist) that are seeking to create confusion and misinformation of BLM (Corley, 2021).

The next section will involve a review of left-wing extremist groups that have a long history of engaging in violent activities so that their ideological positions are promoted within the United States.

ECO-TERRORISM AND ANIMAL RIGHTS EXTREMISM

When we examine the various characteristics of eco-terrorist and animal extremist groups in the United States, we must view these organizations as special interest groups. Based on their ideology and the behavior of each group, they differ from the traditional left-wing and right-wing terrorist groups (Lewis, 2004). As illustrated in the Weathermen Underground (also referred to as the Weather Underground) case study, these special interest groups are focused on resolving specific issues that are collectively viewed as being unacceptable in society. These groups are primarily leaderless, can be violent, and engage in various criminal and domestic terrorism activities to support their organizational goals. For example, there are many instances where both the Animal Liberation Front (ALF) and the Earth Liberation Front (ELF) have engaged in bombings and acts of arson (Benda, 2021). Other nonviolent activities, also known as **monkeywrenching**, involve the use of civil disobedience and sabotage that contributes to achieving the ideological goals of the group. A review of the ALF and ELF organizations will help illustrate the various eco-terrorism and animal rights extremists and how they differ from a traditional left-wing extremist ideology.

The Animal Liberation Front

The ALF was established in Great Britain in the mid-1970s due to an ongoing observance of animal abuse and exploitation (Lewis, 2004). This organization lacks a defined structure, and it presents a philosophy in which membership can be attained through an individual or group action that is focused on protecting the welfare of animals (Lewis, 2004). As noted by Chermak et al. (2013), ALF extremists were more likely to conduct isolated attacks on individuals and organizations that have some involvement in animal exploitation. Most of these attacks were focused on animal research facilities and corporations that contributed to the harm of animals; corporations that tested beauty products on animals were highly targeted. One of the most significant attacks conducted by an ALF member was when Rodney Coronado went to the Michigan State University campus in 1992 and set a makeshift firebomb to explode in the office Richard Aulerich, a university researcher who Coronado believed was conducting research that was funded by the commercial fur industry (Wolcott, 2017). According to Wolcott (2017), while no one was hurt from the explosion, the goal was to create a psychological impact that would make any researchers involved in animal testing to think twice about their safety.

The Earth Liberation Front

ELF, a decentralized and underground extremist group, was established in California in 1996 (Loadenthal, 2014). As with the ALF, members of ELF have engaged in clandestine activities; however, this group has been focused on attacking "soft targets," such as vehicles, phone booths, and constructions sites (Loadenthal, 2014, p. 23). The organization is active in 14 countries across the continents of North America, South America, Europe, and Australia (Loadenthal, 2014, p. 27). As outlined by McKee (2022), one of the worst eco-terrorist attacks that occurred in the United States was when members of ELF committed arson against the Vail Ski Resort in Colorado. The attack was in response to the resort having plans to expand its footprint in the area; ELF argued that this expansion endangered the lynx that was indigenous to that area. The damage from the attack was over $10 million, and 6 of the 7 individuals involved in the attack have been imprisoned.

SUMMARY

There will likely always be an ongoing threat of left-wing and right-wing extremist ideologies within the United States. While the left-wing threat has been less active over the past 20 years, they still possess the capability and motivation to fight for their particular ideology. The U.S. government has stated that White supremacy is an issue, but they have not named any affiliated groups terrorists. However, the right-wing groups have become more abundant and pose an immediate threat. White supremacy is not leaving the United States in the near future. The fight for equality will continue.

REVIEW QUESTIONS

Directions: Based on what you have learned in this chapter, respond to the questions and prompts below.

1. How do religion and racism intersect in White supremacy groups?
2. How has politics influenced the popularity and capabilities of right-wing extremist groups?
3. Considering the circumstances that surrounded the 2021 U.S. Capitol riot, do you believe this was simply a peaceful event that turned violent or was it a result of right-wing extremist influence leading to violence?

FIGURE CREDITS

Fig. 3.1: Source: https://www.fbi.gov/image-repository/klan-march-dc.jpeg/view.

Fig. 3.2: Source: https://catalog.archives.gov/id/535792.

Fig. 3.3: Copyright © by TapTheForwardAssist (CC BY-SA 4.0) at https://commons.wikimedia.org/wiki/File:DC_Capitol_Storming_IMG_7965.jpg.

CHAPTER 4

Financing Terrorism

GUIDING QUESTIONS

- What are the ideologies of the Al-Qaeda, ISIS, FARC, and Taliban terrorist organizations?
- What are the sources of funding for terrorist organizations?
- What is human trafficking?

INTRODUCTION

The United States government has multiple definitions for terrorism, depending on whether you read the definition of the U.S. State Department, the U.S. Justice Department, or the U.S. Treasury Department. Each speaks to the general idea that terrorism is the use of violence against others to create political or social change. None of the definitions of terrorism address the organization's motivation to exist and to prosper.

Terrorism is not just about ideology and a political position; terrorism is a business. As is true with any business, you either make money to support the expenses of purchasing products, maintaining your infrastructure, and paying your employees or you go out of business. It is important that we look at these issues in order to understand and combat terrorist activities. Within Chapter 4, we will look at the historical formation and actions of terrorist organizations, international laws related to these groups, terrorist use of and trends in technology, and methods of funding, recruitment, and communication.

KEY TERMS

- terrorist financing
- human trafficking
- terrorist organization

TERRORIST ORGANIZATIONS AND THEIR IDEOLOGY

In order to better explore the relationship of terrorism and transnational organized crime, we will focus on four well-known **terrorist organizations**: Al-Qaeda, ISIS, FARC, and the Taliban. Three are classic Middle Eastern, Muslim-based groups, and one is from South America. The oldest is FARC (Fuerzas Armadas Revolucionarias de Colombia [Revolutionary Armed Forces of Colombia]), designated by the U.S. State Department in October of 1997 (Bureau of Counterterrorism and Countering Violent Extremism, n.d.). Al-Qaeda was labeled in 1999 and Taliban/Tehrik-e Taliban Pakistan (TTP) in 2010, but the more well-known Taliban in Afghanistan remains off the list of designated terrorist organizations for more political than ideological reasons (Farivar, 2017). ISIS/ISIL was listed with terrorist organizations in 2004 under the name Al-Qa`ida in Iraq, renaming itself in 2006, according to the U.S. State Department (Bureau of Counterterrorism and Countering Violent Extremism, n.d.). Each group formed for different reasons and from different experiences and has evolved in their reasoning and methodologies.

FARC formed as a response to the economic disparities existing in Colombia and the attempt by the government and private land owners to break apart rural farming collectives they saw as a threat. At the height of the organization, FARC had a membership of over 20,000 armed combatants. FARC's beginning as a disparate group of farmers gathering to resist the forces of the Colombian government meant that they could live off the support of local communities and their own farming. As time passed and the numbers grew along with the logistical requirements of taking the fight to the Colombian government, the need for finances grew.

Al-Qaeda, through Bin Laden, focused on uniting the Arab/Muslim world and creating a society based on the strict beliefs of Salafism. The belief that anyone allowing nonbelievers onto Muslim soil was a traitor was espoused by Al-Qaeda leadership. This belief allowed them to justify a call to overthrow governments like that of Saudi Arabia and to establish a "declaration of jihad" against the West, primarily America as we were seen to be an invading force (Blanchard, 2007). To support this belief, the leaders of Al-Qaeda would refer to acts of aggression from the West and the United States against individuals that were Muslim or in countries that were identified as being Muslim. This imagery was supported with historical reminders of the invasion and killings from outside armies occurring during the Crusades. Once Bin Laden had the focus of Muslims that supported his point of view, he needed the funds to wage his jihad of defense.

Osama Bin Laden came from a wealthy Saudi family, which had a reported net worth of $7 billion dollars in 2009 (Frank, 2009), and his personal net worth was estimated at between $50 and $300 million dollars, as was reported by Kenneth Katzman, a member of the Congressional Research Service (Levin, 2001). Although these funds might have been available for use in aiding Al-Qaeda, the primary money gained by Osama Bin Laden was through his fundraising for the organization. Just how much money was used by the terrorist organizations is unknown specifically, but some data exists on their revenues.

As an example, Marc Chernick (2007) identifies the annual budget for FARC to be between $100 million and $1 billion dollars annually, while Afghan Taliban took in between $240 million and $360 million dollars a year, according to research by Peter Kenyon (2010), (Freeman, 2011). So how does an organization obtain the finances necessary to maintain annual budgets of this size? Simply put, they commit crimes and participate in illegal activities.

SOURCES OF TERRORIST FINANCING

Terrorist financing can be broken down into four primary sources: legal activities, illegal activities, state sponsorship, and individual support. State sponsorship will not be addressed here as it is less of an issue as related to transnational criminal organizations.

LEGAL SOURCES OF INCOME

The legal sources of terrorist financing can be seen in groups like Al-Qaeda, which operated a variety of businesses in the Sudan in the early to mid-90s, including honey and furniture production, peanut farming, a bakery, and an investment company (Burke, 2007). Other branches of Al-Qaeda ran construction, manufacturing, and plumbing companies to create legitimate income, according to Paul Smith, (Forest, 2007). Although completely legal sources of income, the relationship to transnational criminal activities becomes apparent when we see how the money is moved and the funds are used. Unlike traditional criminal enterprises that seek to hide how money is made, terrorist organizations are less concerned with how they make their money and more about how they move the funds and what those funds are spent on. However, not all sources of income are as legitimate, and when the income source is related to illegal activities, you quickly start to see similarities between funding sources for terrorism and criminal organizations. Terrorist groups use criminal organizations for the skills and resources they provide in logistics, money laundering, and distribution of illegal products and proceeds. The types of illegal activities vary between terrorist groups, based on the needs and abilities within their organization and what works given their proximity to resources.

ILLEGAL SOURCES OF INCOME

Crime in general is an easy and repeatable source of income, depending on your knowledge of the crime occurring. Picarelli and Shelley state that the benefit of crime is that "crime provides cash on a rapid and repeatable basis" (Giraldo & Trinkunas, 2007). How much cash is created through these illegal activities and which activities terrorists pursue vary, but crime does pay. As Freeman points out, the criteria that need to be evaluated when picking a source of income are "quantity, legitimacy, security, reliability, control and simplicity" (2011, p. 463). Picking the right source of income impacts one or all of these factors and the potential benefits to the organization.

Drug Trafficking

According to the 2003 report given by the Senate Judiciary Committee to Congress, 14 of the 36 organizations identified as terrorist groups participated in drug trafficking (Tofangsaz, 2015). To better understand the relationship between drugs and terrorism, we will look at the impact of drugs as a funding source for two organizations: FARC and the Taliban. FARC, in Colombia, has used the farming, production, transportation, and sale of coca/cocaine as a significant source of income in the past. According to the United Nations Office on Drugs and Crime World Drug Report, Colombia was responsible for producing 640 metric tons of cocaine, or 70% of the world's production of cocaine, in 2005 (2006). In 2004, over 400 tons of cocaine were exported with a domestic value of $2 billion (UNODC, 2005). While the exact numbers earned by FARC are unknown, the amount would be significant even at a 2%–5% share of production; they would make $40–$100 million from cocaine production and sale alone. However, the ability to make money from drugs is not a unidimensional process. Terrorist organizations may be responsible for growing coca and opium, providing manpower to process or guard growing and production facilities, giving transportation security, and also collecting transportation taxes imposed to allow drivers and traffickers to move freely on roads controlled by the organization—all sources of income (Freeman, 2011).

In 2006 Afghanistan opium traffickers had gross profits of $2.34 billion, and the export value to neighboring countries totaled $3.1 billion (UNODC, 2007). The Taliban's share of these profits between 2003 and 2008 totaled between $90 and $160 million per year (Kenyon, 2010). In the neighboring country of Turkey, the Partiya Karkeren Kurdistane, or PKK as they are better known, is also heavily involved in the drug trade. Estimates suggest that as many as three quarters of the drugs available in Europe connect to the PKK (Roth & Sever, 2007). They also are significantly involved in smuggling people into Europe, primarily through Italy, at the cost of approximately $2,000–$3,000 dollars per person. One such operation involved smuggling 9,000 Kurdish individuals, potentially making the PKK $20–$30 million (Roth & Sever, 2007). And smuggling is not limited to people: Terrorist organizations have smuggled almost anything, including people, gems, animals, cigarettes, cash, and drugs (Freeman, 2011). In addition to smuggling, terrorists will use other sources of illegal financing.

Kidnapping and Extortion

Activities such as extortion of individuals, businesses, and conglomerates have occurred. Freeman cites the work of Loretta Napolleoni (2003), which says some of this extortion included the PLO (Palestine Liberation Organization), which extorted $5 to $10 million a year from airlines in the 1970s along with the alleged extortion of the Organization of the Petroleum Exporting Countries (OPEC) to the amount of $100 to $220 million (2011).

Kidnapping is also a common enterprise. With kidnapping, the terrorist organization gets the opportunity to use the individual for multiple purposes. These can include holding them for ransom, which was done by the Montoneros of Argentina for a record $60 million as reported in a 2001 book by Paul Lewis (Freeman, 2010). The ability to create fear in the population or in local or national governments and also in foreign companies operating in the terrorist's territory makes kidnapping a valuable tool as well. This fear may lead to cooperation from the populace or capitulating by local police and political groups that avoid passing or enforcing laws in certain regions. When the government fails to protect the citizenry and laws are not enforced, the message to the populace is that the government is not in power, and they become an illegitimate institution. This dissolution of legitimacy can lead companies to withdraw their investments or withhold their capital, harming the economy and reinforcing the image that the terrorists are a legitimate organization and that the government is corrupt and impotent. These issues have played out in Colombia and in areas of Mexico where the drug cartels use these methods to control the territory needed to maintain their criminal enterprises.

Kidnapping an individual can serve an even darker purpose. Sometimes these kidnappings are not done for financial gain but instead to control a political agenda through intimidation and removal of political opposition. This was the case in Mexico prior to their 2018 elections. As reported in their national registry in the month of May, 2,890 people were killed, which averages 93 people a day, and over 100 individuals running for office who have not agreed to look the other way in cartel-related business were killed in the roughly six months leading up to the elections (Turak, 2018). Many of these messages were general, but some were specific, such as the ISIS beheading of journalist James Foley, in a video where the terrorist says his execution was in response to the American presence in Iraq (Carter, 2014). Kidnapping and extortion are easily reproduced sources of income. Also, they serve political purposes, but other sources of income have a far greater return on investment for one group in particular.

Oil and Gas

ISIS gained much of its power and financial strength through the control of the regions in Iraq and Syria that had oil and natural gas production. It was the focus of ISIS to effectively use and expand the existing oil and gas production of territories it controlled, increase production and sales to generate income for the organization, and lastly to seize production facilities and control transportation of resources in an effort to punish and weaken the economic standing of Western states (Tichy, 2019). ISIS expanded its control of territory and used this control to generate tremendous revenues. Sources of revenue are a constant focus for many terrorist organizations as many rely on others to fund their activities. If they engage in behavior that their supporters do not approve of, they can remove their financial resources and cripple the ability of the group to promote their agenda, plan and execute terrorist events, and pay the members of the organization. Just as is true with any business, you must be able to pay your employees, cover your overhead, promote your product or service, and deliver your goods—otherwise customers will find another source. Lack of funding has impacted the ability of many terrorist organizations to solidify their existence or maintain their relevancy. It is not unusual to hear of other terrorist groups pledging allegiance to ISIS, in part due to the financial strength it was able to create.

During 2014, ISIS managed to gain control over vast expanses of the Syrian and Iraqi oil and gas production lands. These areas included 60% of the Syrian oil production and 10% of the production in Iraq, resulting in oil production between $2 and $4 million daily, or $700 million to almost $1.5 billion annually (Brisard & Martinez, 2014). Through a strategy to take back land, particularly those that generated the oil production of ISIS, by 2017 the international community was able to significantly impact the power and presence of the organization and reduce their prior production of $4 million daily to that amount monthly (Tichy, 2018). Although ISIS is much more of a self-funded organization than many terrorist groups, it still needs to remember those prior resource goals and maintain sources of financing that are able to preserve "quantity, legitimacy, security, reliability, control, and simplicity" (Freeman, 2011). As the revenues from oil and gas have receded, ISIS has been required to look toward other sources, and the instability within the country of Libya has become an area of interest. However, it still has resources within its control. One such resource is heavily concentrated in their area of operation and represents the history of the region: antiquities.

Antiquities

According to the Center for Environmental Management of Military Lands, Interpol reports that the smuggling and sale of antiquities is one of the top five organized criminal activities worldwide (n.d.) The routes that ISIS uses to smuggle antiquities out of their territory are the same routes being used for smuggling drugs, oil, and gas, or any other illicit product and for human trafficking. Many of these routes existed prior to the formation of ISIS and are used by nonterrorist organizations. These are transnational criminal enterprises that profit from the acquisition, transportation, sale, and delivery of cultural heritage throughout the world. Not only are these items of value, but estimated annual trade also approximates $7 billion annually (De Groote & Dewaele, 2009). Part of the appeal in trafficking antiquities for groups like ISIS or Al-Qaeda is again the ease of using these as methods of creating revenue. People that look for, find, and recover these ancient artifacts are often made to pay a tax for safe transport across roadways in the form of an Islamic khums tax, based on the value of the artifacts being found, transported, or sold. A khums tax is based on the profit or spoils of war that one has and generally amounts to 20% of the value (Al-Islam.org). These taxes provide an income to the organization, but the sale of artifacts—whether they are art, statues, jewelry, or written documents—all benefit the terrorist organizations in other ways as well. First, they serve to remind the world that the country being looted and the governments responsible for maintaining possession of its wealth and history are incapable of doing their job. Secondly, because so many of the antiquities on the world market—according to Bitterman (2012), roughly 80%—lack sufficient documentation to prove either lawful purchase or ownership history, groups like ISIS can profit from their transportation, sale, and the ability to move them publicly from one area to another without the authorities intervening. ISIS profits on the sale of antiquities have been estimated to be in the mid $30 million dollar range (Lehr & Herdrich, 2014). The sale of these antiquities and artifacts has terrorist organizations interacting with the mafias that control these illegal markets worldwide (Losson, 2017). Whether used by terrorists or trafficking organizations, the transnational criminal value of art makes it an ideal commodity. Art makes a great tool for money laundering and transfers in addition to its salable value.

Money Laundering

Art and artifacts can be transferred in public, and values can be identified as either higher or lower in actual value, depending on what meets the current needs of the trafficking organization. This reality makes art a unique asset to move across national and international borders. When you cannot prove an item's actual value, then the value is set by the owner or the buyer. This reality makes art the perfect medium for money laundering. This is where terrorists have learned from criminal organizations and taken the sale of illicitly obtained artifacts to a new level by looting sacred and ancient sites in war-torn regions around the world. Imagine this scenario: A terrorist organization acquires an item worth $100,000 to a buyer and wants to transfer this item. Often in the case of art, showing ownership is not possible unless the item has already been tracked from prior sales. So they can send the item from Syria to France, and in France, the item will be paid for by a buyer. Where is the money delivered? The answer is in France. If a terrorist needs money in France for a planned event, how would they have been able to receive money overseas from Syria to France without the international banking laws trying to identify the source of the funds, movement through the system, and the end recipient? What about moving cash or precious metals or jewels across international borders? Again, the seller risks detection and has a need to prove ownership. But if art is sold in France, the money is already in France, and the value has been created, allowing organizations to hide illegal transactions. We could claim a value of $1,000, and the buyer would accept the art as payment for other resources—perhaps housing, logistical support, weapons, cars, or whatever is needed for the planned event to happen. Sellers could also value the item at $1,000,000 and thereby allow an individual to transfer the additional $900,000 without showing a donation to the organization, protecting individual supporters from being tracked or shown as terrorist supporters. Passas shares how a terrorist financer may provide a commodity at a lower price, allowing it to be resold and the profit kept for terroristic purposes (2007). It is a basic shell game that can be played in the light instead of in the dark, where many criminal organizations are forced to move their funds. Art transfer is not the only method of moving money that makes it difficult for authorities to track, nor the only currency available to pay for items.

Hawala

In both the past and present, ancient trading routes and systems of communication have allowed for the development and transfer of wealth between people and businesses. These systems were built on trust and anonymity. According to Kiser (2005), often, there may not be an actual transfer of money but rather value instead (Tofangsaz, 2015). This process makes tracking funds even more difficult because many of the money lenders are not registered, and they do not report the transactions between their clients. The most widely known version of this is the hawala, which is used in many Muslim countries but also exists in similar forms in areas of Africa and Asia. An additional benefit to the hawala system beyond not having to transfer money over distances is that the funds are sent and transferred without the receiver knowing the sender, nor the sender knowing the person who receives them. Hawalas have been used to move money for Hamas, Jemaah Islamiyah, and others (Passas, 2007). The use of a hawala keeps the level of anonymity high and protects terrorists or other criminal organizations from the backtracing of money transfers by the authorities. The desire to stay out of the light of law enforcement agencies is a necessity for organizations that are either criminal or terrorist, and the hawala system helps to make that happen. Often the hawala banker has not been told who the beneficiaries are, and this anonymity adds to the interest in using this type of money transfer (Teichmann, 2018). However, the hawala system is not the only system used to send and receive money in an attempt to hide the sender, receiver, and monies from the prying eyes of national and international law enforcement agencies.

Cryptocurrencies

According to a 2015 Europol report, Bitcoin was used in more than 40% of payments between criminals as part of their illegal activities (Malik, 2018). Criminal and terrorist organizations share the desire to move money safely and to hide the parties and processes used to move those funds. Terrorists look for strategies to move funds from where they were collected to where they can be held and then moved to members that need the funds to support themselves and to carry out their terrorist plans (Vittori, 2011). Whereas most criminal organiziations are concerned with hiding the source of their funding (as it is from illegal activities), terrorist organizations are more concerned with hiding the destination of their funds. Once obtained, holding and transferring the funds is more important to terrorist groups so that they can implement their plans and keep authorities from knowing who the end users of the funds are or for what they have been using the funds. From a criminal perspective, the advent of cryptocurrencies—and specifically bitcoin—has provided a tremendous opportunity. Money can be entered into the bitcoin chains, blocked (or added to) other account deposits, and then moved and connected to yet other chains before being separated and arriving at the end source. Because the monies are virtual, it is possible to buy and sell coins without having to interact with banks. Also, the money can be deposited and withdrawn under the safety of encrypted codes that make the funds virtually impossible to trace or track. Money can be deposited almost anywhere and opened up across the world in minutes, much like an email. This allows for rapid deployment of funds to cell members, who can then use them to pay for any number of needs, from housing and food to buying supplies. This makes bitcoin and cryptocurrencies, in general, an integral part of the world of those organizations that benefits them immensely.

SEX TRAFFICKING OF LGBTQ TEENS

This content is authored by Dale Yeager, who holds a degree in forensic science and is a graduate of the NATO counterterrorism and intelligence programs and the Federal Law Enforcement Training Center DLP program.[1] Mr. Yeager's research work on violence has been published in the FBI Law Enforcement Bulletin and the book *Profiling Violent Crimes: An Investigative Tool* by Dr. Ronald Holmes. Mr. Yeager is a frequent expert with media outlets, including a featured episode of *Forensic Files* and the History Channel series *True Monsters*. Since 1995, Mr. Yeager has served as a federal law enforcement instructor and advisor for the High-Intensity Drug Trafficking Areas (HIDTA) and the Middle Atlantic–Great Lakes Organized Crime Law Enforcement Network (MAGLOCLEN) programs. His content within this chapter is designed to provide background and current data on the crime of human trafficking of juveniles in Southern California. This chapter is not designed to be a comprehensive examination of the issue but an advisory and planning tool for law enforcement.

THE ISSUE

The issue of human trafficking has been a constant throughout the history of the United States, beginning with the enslavement of people to the multinational organized human trafficking of today. Today, the transnational crime of modern-day human trafficking is growing and has become a key concern for all levels of law enforcement. The focus of this chapter will be the sex trafficking of LGBTQ adolescents in Southern California. This subcategory of victims is a unique segment of human sex trafficking and requires customized actions to effectively prevent or prosecute it.

HUMAN TRAFFICKING IN THE UNITED STATES

According to the California Department of Justice, the United States is widely regarded as a destination country for human trafficking. Federal reports have estimated that 14,500 to 17,500 victims are trafficked into the United States annually. This does not include the number of victims who are trafficked within the United States each year.

- States with highest numbers of reported human trafficking cases
  - » California
  - » Texas
  - » Florida

- Top venues/industries for sex trafficking
  - » Illicit massage/spa business

1 Dale Yeager, "Sex Trafficking of LGBQT Teens; Financing Continued." Copyright © by Dale Yeager. Reprinted with permission.

    - Pornography
    - Residence-based commercial sex

- Gender
    - Males
    - Females
    - Gender minorities

- Citizenship
    - Equal percentage of foreign nationals and U.S. citizens

- Age
    - 22.5% are minors

Human trafficking is a crime that involves exploiting a person for labor, services, or commercial sex. The Trafficking Victims Protection Act of 2000 and its subsequent reauthorizations define human trafficking:

1. Sex trafficking in which a commercial sex act is induced by force, fraud, or coercion, or in which the person induced to perform such act has not attained 18 years of age; or
2. The recruitment, harboring, transportation, provision, or obtaining of a person for labor or services, through the use of force, fraud, or coercion for the purpose of subjection to involuntary servitude, peonage, debt bondage, or slavery. (22 U.S.C. § 7102(9)).

HUMAN TRAFFICKING IN CALIFORNIA

California is one of the largest sites of human trafficking in the United States. In 2018, 1,656 cases of human trafficking were reported in California. Of those cases, 1,226 were sex trafficking cases, 151 were labor trafficking cases, and 110 involved both labor and sex trafficking. In 169 cases, the type of trafficking was not specified (Camarillo, 2020). As codified in the California Penal Code, anyone who deprives or violates the personal liberty of another with the intent to obtain forced labor or services, procure or sell the individual for commercial sex, or exploit the individual in obscene matter is guilty of human trafficking. Depriving or violating a person's liberty includes as Camarillo (2020) stated, "substantial and sustained restriction of another's liberty accomplished through fraud, deceit, coercion, violence, duress, menace, or threat of unlawful injury to the victim or to another person, under circumstances where the person receiving or apprehending the threat reasonably believes that it is likely that the person making the threat would carry it out." However, sex trafficking of juveniles is separately defined as "causing, inducing, persuading, or attempting to cause, induce or persuade a minor to engage in a commercial sex act." California is a focal point for trafficking because of its "proximity to international borders, number of ports and airports, significant immigrant population, and large economy that includes industries that attract forced labor" (Camarillo, 2020). It also serves both as an entry point for slaves imported from outside the United States, as well as a destination for slaves, with major hubs centered in Los Angeles, Sacramento, San Diego, and San Francisco.

SEX TRAFFICKING OF LESBIAN, GAY, BISEXUAL, AND TRANSGENDER INDIVIDUALS

A report by Omar Martinez of the HIV Center for Clinical and Behavioral Studies at the New York State Psychiatric Institute and Columbia University details the unique issue of sex trafficking of LGBTQ people (Martinez & Kelle, 2013). Sex trafficking of those in the LBGTQ+ community is commonly overlooked and rarely reported by local and national governments. The underreporting of sex trafficking among this population makes it difficult to understand the specific nature of the crimes and the total number of people affected. Taking this into consideration, this article summarizes some of the limited data available regarding the challenges and issues affecting LGBTQ victims of sex trafficking.

While a majority of victims of human trafficking are domestically trafficked, i.e., forced into labor for another's profit within their own countries by persons of the same nationality, those who are trafficked beyond borders go through a migration process. Examples of documented migration cases include Caribbean and Latin Americans in the LGBTQ community ending up in Western Europe and African victims being found in Europe (particularly Scotland). Other Africans end up in Arab Gulf–based trafficking rings as sex slaves for the wealthy in United Arab Emirates, Qatar, and Saudi Arabia.

LGBTQ individuals are effectively prevented from accessing the outside world. Due to the hidden nature of same-sex prostitution and the stigma associated with being LGBTQ, LGBTQ sex trafficking is even less likely than trafficking in heterosexuals to be reported to local authorities. In addition, immigration status and the anti-immigration rhetoric in the local jurisdiction add to public health and legal concerns of victims. As a result, LGBTQ individuals fall into political and social traps that require focused attention from legal and health professionals. The trafficking of gay men is a serious issue with its own particular set of difficulties. Because sexual violence against males is considered taboo in most societies, many male victims are constrained by societal barriers from reporting their ordeals. Environmental factors contribute to the lack of reporting, including the absence of services available for men.

LGBTQ victims face unique and distinct health challenges. These challenges include physical trauma from torture and daily mental abuse, which results in profound depression and anxiety; substance abuse problems; physical and domestic violence; and exposure to tuberculosis and communicable diseases, including HIV. In fact, sex trafficking has been linked to the spread of HIV/AIDS. This link has important consequences for individuals and overall public health policies. Forced into commercial sex work, LGBTQ individuals who are trafficked are at high risk of contracting sexually transmitted diseases, which increases the risk for contracting HIV. Sex trafficking victims are also often subject to violent or dangerous sex practices that allow the virus to enter the body more easily. Sex trafficking has additionally been associated with contributing to new strains of the virus that are resistant to treatment. More research, health promotion, and awareness are needed to address the wide range of health disparities affecting LGBTQ victims of sex trafficking.

LGBTQ Youth and Sex Trafficking

At first glance, adolescents who work in the commercial sex industry may be identified as prostitutes. As prostitution is illegal in most countries, adolescents may initially be labeled as criminals. However, since sex trafficking and prostitution involve the sale of sex and sexual acts, adolescents are actually, according to the legal criteria, the victims of criminal activity, i.e., of sex trafficking. Specifically, adolescents who are forced into commercial sex acts through the use of coercion, fraud, or threats are considered victims of sex trafficking regardless of their age, and any person younger than age 18 involved in any form of commercial sexual exploitation (e.g., prostitution, pornography, sex tourism, and stripping) is considered the victim of the crime of sex trafficking of a minor.

The legal criteria or definitions, which provide additional legal protection to victims, are provided under the Trafficking Victims Protection Act, which was adopted by the U.S. Congress in 2000 and reauthorized and revised in 2003, 2005, and 2008 (Siskin A., C & Wyler, 2012).

Aside from being illegal, crimes committed against child trafficking victims (e.g., threats, extortion, theft of documents or property, false imprisonment, aggravated or sexual assault, pimping, rape, and murder) result in an immeasurable amount of short- and long-term physical, mental, and emotional harm. Minors are targeted more frequently because they are easy to manipulate and unable to protect themselves.

LGBTQ Youth at Risk of Sex Trafficking

LGBTQ minors who are homeless are at the highest risk for sex trafficking and sexual exploitation. According to the U.S. National Coalition for the Homeless (www.nationalhomeless.org), homeless LGBTQ youth are much more vulnerable to sexual exploitation and trafficking than other homeless youths. For instance, only 20% of homeless youth are LGBTQ in the United States, and 58.7% of them are exploited through sexual prostitution. This is a much higher rate than the 33.4% of heterosexual homeless youth at risk of sexual exploitation on the street (Martinez & Kelle, 2013).

Nearly 40% of homeless youth identify as LGBTQ, compared to 7% of the general population (Martinez & Kelle, 2013). These youth may face homelessness for reasons connected to their identities, such as family rejection, prior abuse or neglect, bullying in school, or social discrimination and marginalization. Youth without safe shelter and social support are at higher risk of trafficking and exploitation. Traffickers exploit their needs and vulnerabilities to compel them into sex or labor trafficking. LGBTQ youth may be trafficked by intimate partners, family members, friends, or strangers. The coercion and control those traffickers hold over their victims, combined with the stigma of commercial sex, may prevent youth from disclosing their situation. LGBTQ youth service providers may be in a unique position to recognize indicators of sex trafficking among those they serve and connect them with needed services.

Lack of reporting limits the ability to protect LGBTQ youth. If local publications and news channels do not report on the prevalence of human trafficking and the disproportionate number of homeless and runaway youth that are LGBTQ, it creates a perception that LGBTQ human trafficking and youth homelessness are issues outside the community. Increasing awareness of the worldwide prevalence of such issues will lead to a productive societal debate as to how we might constructively address the core issues affecting LGBTQ homeless youth.

SUMMARY

Law enforcement leaders must make a concerted effort to reach out to the LGBTQ adolescents in their communities for intelligence related to human trafficking. Planning for prevention and interdiction requires constant intelligence updates. By controlling human trafficking, law enforcement will be able to reduce violent crimes.

SCENARIO

Create a one-page APA formatted document including seven to 10 references to support your answer to the following question: If you were a law enforcement professional tasked with preventing human trafficking in your jurisdiction, how would you plan for prevention and interdiction by working with intelligence updates provided?

APPENDIX A. *SICARIO* MOVIE ESSAY

Sicario is a crime thriller starring Emily Blunt, Josh Brolin, and John Bernthal (Villeneuve, 2015). Watch the movie and answer the following questions in essay *format (two to three paragraphs to support your answers with five to seven references in APA format)*:

1. What is the reason for the state department to "pull an agent"?
2. Why did the CIA attach itself to domestic agencies to include the FBI on the task force?
3. Who was used as bait in the film *Sicario*?
4. Which Mexican city do they talk about in the trailer?
5. To find him would be like discovering a ________.

6. Who is the director of the film *Sicario*?
7. Which actress in the movie *Sicario* has won a Golden Globe?
8. Who is the writer of the film *Sicario*?
9. Why is this movie important to watch for the intelligence collection/organized crime elements?
10. What does "sicario" mean, exactly?
11. What's the story behind that "NO MORE WEAPONS!" sign at the border?
12. *Sicario* asks us questions of morality: How far is too far? To fight such monstrous evil, is it necessary to become evil ourselves?
13. When we rightly look away in horror as the vicious acts of real-life cartels are splashed across the news, does it make sense to pay to be entertained by such insanity perpetrated by fictional cartels as their dirty deeds are splashed across movie screens?
14. The audience is reminded of Nietzsche's words of warning, "whoever fights monsters should see to it that in the process he does not become a monster." What did he mean by this warning?

SUMMARY

We learned that terrorism is not just about ideology and a political position; terrorism is a business. As is true with any business, you either make money to support the expenses of purchasing products, maintaining your infrastructure, and paying your employees or you go out of business. It is essential that we look at these issues in order to understand and combat terrorist activities. Within Chapter 4, we looked at the historical formation and actions of terrorist organizations, international laws related to these groups, terrorist use of and trends in technology, and methods of funding, recruitment, and communication.

CHAPTER 5

America's Cyber Insecurity

Our technological powers increase, but the side effects and potential hazards also escalate.

— Alvin Toffler

Technological progress is like an axe in the hands of a pathological criminal.

— Albert Einstein

GUIDING QUESTIONS

- What is cyberspace?
- What is cybercrime?
- What is cyberstalking?

INTRODUCTION

With advancement in technology, the criminal landscape has evolved and transcended the physical into the electronic realm, even with terrorist organizations such as Al-Qaeda and ISIS using electronic means to fund their activities. The term *cybercrime*, for example, is a symbolic reference to "online insecurity and risk, widely used to describe the crimes or harms that are committed using networked technologies" (Wall, 2010, p. 89). Cybercrime has become the vehicle for the modern manifestation of crime, with those engaging in such digital intrusions doing so individually or even in organized groups (Barua, 2008). This chapter seeks to address the cyberspace internet world and its relationship to crime, with particular emphasis on (a) its impact on offender motive and modus operandi, (b) multiple manifestations of crime inclusive of organized crime, (c) criminal profiles, (d) digital forensics in cybercrime scene investigations and, (e) policing the internet.

KEY TERMS

- cyberspace
- cybercrime
- cyberstalking
- transnational organized crime

CRIMINALS IN CYBERSPACE

Unregulated interdependence, digital connectivity, and deterritorialization have become hallmarks of the modern era of capitalist cyberculture and the continued globalization in which *e-criminality* thrives (Sandywell, 2010). **Cybercrime** has many definitive characteristics, especially given the advent of **cyberspace**, with offenses ranging from copyright infringement to "at the highest level, cyberterrorism against a whole society information structure" (Sandywell, 2010, p. 45). Cyberspace has become a war zone where the prized resource is information itself, giving rise to not only identity theft but also to digital hackers capable of crippling organizations and leaking private information. Additionally, those involved are not just limited to rogue digital warriors, but governments, the military, and private organizations all seek information to be used for good or bad.

The method by which cybercriminals commit an offense is deemed their *modus operandi* (MO), and this is distinct from their motive. The criminal act is intertwined with the use or development of technologies to achieve such an act. Victim selection, victim surveillance, stalking, and harassment can all be facilitated through the internet and cyberspace where the offender enjoys the "anonymity or 'facelessness' of cyberspace as an effect of the deterritorialization of social encounters and online relationships (Sandywell, 2010, p. 44). Theft or destruction of assets, as well as locating, storing, and disseminating confidential/illicit material, can likewise be facilitated through the medium of cyberspace (Casey & Turvey, 2011, p. 290). Thus, an offender's *modus operandi*—how they commit the crime and the medium they use—is directly impacted by emerging technology.

Unlike *modus operandi*, motive to commit crime may be completely independent of technology. An offender does not require new technology to have a motive to commit crime. Even in the absence of modern technology, motives to commit crime have existed historically. Technology has influenced *how* the crime is committed, but not necessarily the offender's motivational typology. Motivational typologies may broadly include, but not be limited to, power reassurance (compensatory); power assertive (entitlement); anger retaliatory (anger or displaced); anger excitation (sadistic); or profit oriented (Le, 2012). The following paragraphs will explore each of these typologies.

A power reassurance motivational typology, for example, speaks to a need to restore self-confidence and worth. Although the motivation and means may not be highly aggressive, its manifestation may include "a misguided belief that the victim desires the offences behavior, and is somehow a willing or culpable participant; [or] in the form of self-depreciating or self-loathing behavior which is intended to garner a response of pity sympathy from the victim" (Turvey, 2011, p. 298). The expected result is that the victim will not only "enjoy and eroticize the offence behavior, [but] subsequently fall in love with the offender" (Turvey, 2011, p. 298), and, in so doing, emotionally reassure the offender. A common example of this appears in online relationships that have led to obsessive stalking behaviors.

Power assertion is the polar opposite of reassurance, with the offender seeking more aggressive means to fulfill a need for exercising control and mastery, if not humiliation, of their victim. Yet, as Turvey (2011) explains, the goal is to restore the self-worth and confidence of the offender and is not necessarily aimed at harming the victim as much as "demonstrating power over their victims [as] their means of expressing mastery, strength, control, authority and identity to themselves ... to reinforce the offender's inflated sense of confidence and self-worth" (Turvey, 2011, p. 299).

Retaliation in anger as a response to wrongs or perceived wrongs committed by the victim manifests in actions typically being more violent and brutal as compared to power reassurance and stalking, which may engender levels of low aggression. However, although anger retaliation may be violent, it differs from a sadistic typology in that intentional torture of the victim may not necessarily be involved. Sadistic behavior may have a clear offender sexual gratification component brought about by the victim's pain and suffering. The "sexual expression for the offender is manifested in physical aggression, or torture behavior, toward the victim" (Turvey, 2011, p. 301).

Lastly, profit orientation, as the name suggests, grants some level of material or personal gain. Here, psychological or emotional needs may not be as great a motivator as they are in other behavioral typologies. Nevertheless, profit and financial crimes have evolved through the use of technology where financial banking information can be accessed digitally and exploited, and they result in someone being victimized.

Public perception of cyberspace has been, and continues to be, socially constructed. The internet in particular, "has been constructed culturally as a criminogenic virtual environment as a crime problem in and of itself" (Wall, 2010, p. 100), although the practical reality may be different. Just as public fear of crime often exceeds the reality of crime and its occurrence (Prieto Curiel & Bishop, 2017), cybercrime is no exception. Some theorists question whether cybercrime differs from traditional crime predating the internet or whether it simply evolved as the internet evolved. Others question whether cybercrime is a new type of crime distinct altogether from its predecessors. Regardless of the nascence, law enforcement and criminologists are unsure how to respond to the phenomenon. If it truly is a new crime, "social scientists must identify these new types of crimes and develop new theories or adapt current theories to explain these behaviors ... [as] it is a necessity to have valid theoretical framework to explain cybercrime" (Schaefer,

2014, p. 40). Even the United Nations Office on Drugs and Crime has difficulty creating a standardized definition for organized crime, for example, claiming that the lack of this is "intended to allow for a broader applicability of the UNTOC to new types of crime that emerge constantly as global, regional and local conditions change over time" (UNODC, 2019, p. 1).

Crime's manifestation and evolution into cybercrime occurs in an intangible constructed cyberspace—a technological internet space—that has become intrinsic to modern daily life and society and fueling changes in how we view and interact with the world. The motivational typologies as well as the *modus operandi* supported by the use of technology have allowed for various manifestations of cybercrimes.

Stalking is not a new crime. **Cyberstalking** follows the same basic principles of stalking. The motives are similar, though the *modus operandi* may have evolved. The internet is a tool in the hands of a stalker to further their desires. "Stalkers use the Internet to acquire victims, gather information, monitor victims, hide their identities and avoid capture" (Casey, 2011(a), p. 433). All such activities done prior to the internet's inception have simply been enhanced through the use of the technology. Cyberstalking is simply an extension of the physical form of stalking (Marshall University, 2018). However, it can be argued that through cyberspace interaction, the stalker's behavior may become more depraved.

Cyberstalking allows for perpetrators to be geographically distant from their victim and still commit the crime, which raises questions of jurisdiction to prosecute such criminal cases (Hinduja, 2018). Moreover, continued advancements in technology have created both physical and software devices to further cyberstalking. Micro hidden cameras, microphones, and other devices may be used to capture or record the victim unawares, which can be later posted online or even livestreamed. Once installed, software in the form of spyware can remotely monitor a victim's information on their computer, handheld electronic devices, or cellphones. Although physical contact may not always be involved, thinking of the behavior patterns as "less threatening or less dangerous than physical stalking [is a] misperception [as it can be] as frightening and potentially as dangerous as a stalker at the victim's front door" (Marshall University, 2018, p. 1). In the absence of a stalker's physical presence, the potential torment can be psychological and lead to multilayered physical, emotional, and psychological expressions of trauma for the victim. The results of such trauma may include sleep disturbances, hypervigilance, recurring nightmares, high levels of stress, eating disturbances, a feeling of being out of control, and a pervasive sense of the loss of personal safety (Marshall University, 2018, p. 1). Cyberstalking has also been described as an extension of cyberbullying with multiple similarities to the latter. A "common denominator is [is] that the behavior makes the target extremely concerned for their personal safety and causes some form of distress, fear, or annoyance" (Hinduja, 2018, p. 1). The stalker in such crimes may be known to the victim or have a direct obsession with a particular victim. But not all cybercriminals have personal obsessive interest in their victims or perpetrate the crime independently.

Perhaps even more influential and potentially deadly is crime perpetrated by organized groups. The United Nations Convention on Transnational Organized Crime describes an organized criminal group as "a structured group of three or more persons, existing for a period of time and acting in concert with the aim of committing one or more serious crimes or offences established in accordance with this Convention, in order to obtain, directly or indirectly, a financial or other material benefit" (UNODC, 2004, p. 5). The definition of an organized criminal group opens the door for an implied definition of **transnational organized crime** as one that "encompasses virtually all profit-motivated serious criminal activities with international implications [taking into account] the global complexity of the issue and allow[ing] cooperation on the widest possible range of common concerns" (UNODC, 2019).

Organized crime can have multiple incarnations. Outside of common cybercrimes such as identity theft and cyberstalking, cybercrime attacks can attract the attention of organizations and governments who fear modern-day cyberterrorism. Terrorism can be described as a form of organized crime with criminal group members driven by the organization's mandate and goals. As Denning (2010) asserts, "the Internet has transformed terrorism by adding another means of inflicting harm on non-combatants, namely through cyber-attacks" (p. 198). Cyberterrorism may be perceived on the darker end of the cybercrime spectrum as a result of terrorist involvement.

Terrorism is often viewed as one of the worst crimes and acts of violence that can be perpetrated against civilians, a group, or a nation, leaving not only physical but also psychological wounds that may scar a nation's landscape for generations. The internet has transformed terrorism in many ways. From a cybercrime perspective, terrorist cyberattacks targeting power grids, for example, can cause a power shutdown which in turn can lead to physical or even economic damages. However, for the terrorist perpetrator, the advantages of cyberspace extend beyond cyberattacks. Rather, terrorist cyberattacks may appear more trivial, failing to "produce damages or psychological effects comparable to those by bombings and other acts of violence [but instead] resemble those of other hackers who have nothing to do with terrorism. As a consequence, cyber-terrorism is often dismissed as fear mongering" (Denning, 2010, p. 198). Moreover, some theorists argue that "anxiety over terrorists utilizing the Internet will always support someone's agenda" (Wykes & Harcus, 2010, p. 223). Thus, the fear of crime, including cybercrime, has its place in constructed realities to serve someone's agenda as security against perceived threat of crime is also a profitable market.

Though the cyberattack element of terrorism may appear less than effective or noteworthy when compared to physical, more violent acts of terror, the cyberspace has facilitated the rapid growth and development of this form of crime in the real world. Thus, the influence of cyberspace is not limited to cybercrimes occurring within that medium, but also extends its influence to non-cybercrimes, which have real world consequences of actions committed in cyberspace. Simply put, the internet and its usage have "brought about an expansion of damaging acts in support of terrorist objectives, regardless of whether these acts are characterized as cyber-terrorism or not" (Denning, 2010, p. 198). Yet "despite advantages it offers terrorists, Internet technology has also proved highly beneficial to counter-terrorism efforts" (Wykes & Harcus, 2010, p. 221), suggesting that the internet can be a double-edged sword with its effectiveness or deadliness dependent on its wielder and their motives.

Policing and adequately responding to cybercrime problems, inclusive of organized crime, continues to be a challenge for law enforcement, due in part to factors inclusive of "the transnational scale of the Internet, the sheer scope and variety of online offenses, and lack of resources and technical expertise among criminal justice agencies" (Yar, 2010, p. 546; Jewkes, 2010). In the wake of state policing deficiencies, private profit-motivated policing has risen to the challenge of shouldering the responsibility for a paying customer base. With increases in crime, or rather insecurity and fear of cybercrime, "the commercial (for-profit) provision of goods and services aimed at crime prevention, detection and resolution [as well as] IT security products and services on a commercial basis" (Yar, 2010, p. 550) has risen and become a profitable financial market for private organizations specializing in computer crime control. Crime is profitable, as is the sale of goods and services to prevent or deter crime. "These products and services are variously concerned with safeguarding the integrity of operation of computer systems; controlling access to systems; and protecting data content of systems from theft, unauthorized disclosure, and alteration" (Yar, 2010, p. 550). With such a proliferation of private policing organizations, which by nature may be more difficult to regulate, their legitimacy and democracy come into question. In addition, private policing against cybercrime broadens the potential for further inequality and extension of the divide between those who can and those who cannot afford the necessary protection against such cybercrimes.

SUMMARY

Where state policing is concerned, there is a need for "the appointment of officers with qualifications in computing and related areas ... to change the culture of an institution in urgent need of modernization" (Jewkes, 2010, p. 543). Moreover, such modernization needs to be continual, as "the history of cybercrime is also not static; rather it is driven by the opportunities created by the convergence of networked technologies, which continue to occur" (Wall, 2010, p. 100). As cybercrime continues to evolve, policing it needs to likewise evolve to adequately address both changes and new types of crime. Crime scene investigations have evolved; however, we must also consider digital crime scenes and forensics.

REVIEW QUESTIONS

Directions: Based on what you have learned in this chapter, respond to the questions and prompts below.

1. What is the method by which cybercriminals commit an offense, and what are the threats they pose?
2. Profit and financial crimes have evolved through the use of technology that allows financial banking information to be accessed digitally and exploited, and they result in someone being victimized. Specifically, how has COVID-19 impacted the latter?
3. To change the culture of an institution in urgent need of modernization, how would you implement cyber hygiene?

CHAPTER 6

Military Intelligence Review

Issue Analysis and Recommendations

GUIDING QUESTIONS

- What is military intelligence?
- What is the national dialogue on the issue of combatting terrorism?
- What is political systems theory, and what is group theory?

INTRODUCTION

The importance of military intelligence has been recognized since the beginning of recorded history. The Egyptians had a well-developed secret service, and spying and subversion are mentioned in the Iliad and in the Bible. The ancient Chinese treatise on the art of war devotes much attention to deception and gathering intelligence, arguing that all war is based on deception. In the Middle Ages, political espionage became important. Joan of Arc was betrayed by Bishop Pierre Cauchon of Beauvais, a spy in the pay of the English, and Sir Francis Walsingham developed an effective political spy system for Elizabeth I. During the American Revolution, Nathan Hale and Benedict Arnold achieved fame as spies, and there was considerable use of spies on both sides during the Civil War of the United States.

It is imperative that we have moral individuals within military intelligence. Yet the environment in which members of the military must operate poses a severe threat to consistent moral behavior. In addition to inevitable stresses of leadership in the profession of arms, men and women in uniform in the 21st century face a confusing variety of inconsistencies in national policy, government practice, and social behavior. The state, defended by the military professional, champions the cause of peace while pursuing an open-ended global war on terrorism, supporting protracted military involvements abroad, and providing massive quantities of arms to potential belligerents around the world. The United States government adheres to a strategic nuclear policy that supports nonproliferation but uses nuclear weapons as a threat in pursuing national interests. Defense of American values constitutes the soldier's fundamental purpose, but government officials of the state that embodies those values sometimes deem it necessary to operate pragmatically rather than on the basis of principle. Although society may be ethically better than it was a century ago in that we have more social freedom, more political stability, and a greater degree of equality before the law, along with many other desirable features, we have become a juridical society where trust is minimal and social relations are based on entitlements and legalities. Society demands an ethical military but provides few institutional examples to emulate. Members of the military services swear to support and defend a constitution structured by values, but in our capitalistic society "The laws of the market have ... no ethical norms, and corporations have no consciences" (Greenfield, 2008, p. 427).

KEY TERMS

- military intelligence
- military
- political systems theory
- group theory

DISCUSSION

Military intelligence provides timely, relevant, accurate and synchronized Intelligence and Electronic Warfare (IEW) support to leaders at all levels (tactical war fighting commander to strategic policy makers and the president) across the range of military operations. In war, IEW operations support winning battles and campaigns. In low intensity conflicts, IEW operations support the promotion of peace, the resolution of conflict, and the deterrence of war. These operations reduce uncertainty and risk to U.S. forces and permit effective application of force.

In the following context, intelligence is generally defined as information prepared for the use of policy makers. Such policy makers as generals and presidents take intelligence into account when making their decisions and acting upon them. The information springs from a variety of sources, such as spies or codebreakers, and is analyzed and written by evaluators. The main purpose of intelligence is to enable policy makers to optimize physical and psychological resources. Intelligence sources may be grouped into three categories: human, imagery, and signal.

Human intelligence includes the most basic form of military intelligence, which is observation. Soldiers at the front lines watch their enemies for details that might provide information on what the enemy is doing, as well as where and when and how fast. Soldiers remain the backbone of information about the enemy. The most glamorous, but least reliable source of human intelligence is espionage.

Imagery intelligence is based on visible light, infrared, or radar. Pictures in light give fine detail, while those taken by infrared or radar are coarser but can penetrate darkness or cloud.

They provide literal snapshots of events. Photo interpreters can tell, for instance, how wide a bridge or other structure is.

Signal intelligence is the most important secret intelligence source. It is faster and more dependable than spies, and more insightful than photographs. Signal intelligence obtains information from enemy signals. Radio operators intercept such communications, and teams locate the enemy transmitters. Analysts then diagram the senders and receivers to infer an underlying organization; they graph quantities to predict enemy activity. When codebreakers solve encrypted messages and disclose the actual words of the enemy, they directly reveal enemy capabilities, attitudes, and specific plans.

Intelligence does not win wars. Wars are won by the men and women in the trenches with a commander's ability. But it can help commanders win by optimizing resources. In many instances, intelligence can shorten wars and save lives. Sound decisions depend upon timely, accurate, adequate, and usable information. Wartime decisions carry great responsibility; they affect not only the lives of our fighting men but also the liberty of our people. Decision makers ask questions for which they need answers. In the military, such questions are referred to as essential elements of information (EEI). The number of such important questions should be kept to a minimum. Actually, all decision makers from the commander in chief in the White House to the company commander in the field constantly need extensive information concerning the enemy, terrain, and weather. Their desire for information is insatiable. When American soldiers bivouac in a foreign jungle, their battalion commanders want to know the strength and location of all enemy forces capable of attacking their men during the night—and rightfully so. The list of their questions fills a book very rapidly, and since the situation is always changing, the answers to this book of questions must be kept up-to-date.

Old information needs to be corrected as additional information on the questioned period of time becomes known. Modern communications bring a decision maker in Washington just as close to the source of information as the commander in terms of time. This poses the danger that decisions will be made on information (unevaluated material) and not on intelligence. Information should be evaluated and analyzed before decisions are made on untimely, inaccurate, or inadequate bases. Intelligence must be timely. Time is precious. Decisions made on untimely intelligence can result in disaster if the situation has changed. Intelligence should get to the person who can do something about it in time for him to do something. Timely reporting requires extensive, dedicated communications in support of intelligence. Timeliness also depends upon effectively written messages. In war, communications are overloaded with questions for the originator of information because his initial report was incomplete. Timeliness requires the ability to manipulate data rapidly and assist humans to evaluate it, which only they can do. Computers are a great help, but only that. An automated system of presentation of what a computer "knows" can only reflect a fraction of the database (Greenfield, 2008).

The computer data bank must have tremendous storage capacity and programs to permit timely manipulations. Unless pressure is maintained, promptness will suffer. Each intelligence report should indicate not only distribution made, but when and how each consumer was informed. To ensure that highly perishable reports reach commanders promptly, each headquarters should have an individual whose task is reviewing the reporting process throughout the intelligence cycle. He must read all reports—not for content but for timeliness. He must then ensure that shortcomings are called to the attention of the commanders involved. Commanders and staff officers who ask for more information than they need not only delay the receipt of what they need but frequently cannot use what they receive.

NATIONAL DIALOGUE

The military command in Iraq and Afghanistan has failed and continues to fail to do intelligence collection and analysis adequately in support of the core activities of its combat and counterinsurgency forces in the war. Since the military has failed in that area, it can hardly afford to divide its available resources to do the work it must, per force, see as a secondary set of activities. Why has the U.S. Army's military intelligence establishment been such a failure in Iraq and Afghanistan? What is the evidence of that failure? We cannot defeat the enemy. Counterinsurgency war demands an ability to find among the population the individuals and small groups who are the actual fighters. The exception to this judgment is the application by Special Operations (SO) of massive national intelligence collection means to the pursuit of a small number of "high value" takfiri insurgents like al-Zarqawi (Greenfield, 2008). This SOF effort is only a small part of what the command in Baghdad is supposed to do with its forces. The troops that you see on television in Fallujah, Diyala, the Triangle of Death, etc. are not SOF. They are the main forces; the army brigade combat teams (BCT) and marine regimental combat teams (RCT) who are carrying the main burden of combat. These forces are essentially "fighting blind" against insurgent gunmen, IED implanters, and militia armies. The reason for this is because the U.S. Army has no effective clandestine HUMINT capability in Iraq. There is no *army* (as opposed to DIA or CIA) organization designed to provide information support to maneuver unit commanders. If asked, the army MI establishment will say that they "do" HUMINT (Greenfield, 2008). No, they don't. What they usually mean by HUMINT is talking to someone, often a prisoner. Prisoners are human, but talking to them is not HUMINT in the sense that is generally understood in this context. That is the use of controlled local human agents on their own ground to determine the identity and location of the true effectives among the insurgent enemies.

The U.S. Army is not doing that in Iraq. If pressed on this point, the army and the MI establishment point to what they call Tactical HUMINT Teams (THT). In reality, these teams are made up of counterintelligence people, not espionage operators, and the mission of the teams is that of "force protection" for the particular U.S. combat unit they are part of and with whom they move from place to place. There are several things wrong with the theory and practice involving these teams—the people in the teams are too junior, are not thoroughly trained, and are not led by officers who are themselves skilled HUMINT operators. It is a case of the "blind leading the blind" (Greenfield, 2008). The army no longer trains people adequately for this work, and its policy of making officers managers of the intelligence process—rather than participant leaders—is counter-productive. The THT teams are not engaged in recruiting and running controlled sources. Their sources have not been vetted, trained, and disciplined as would be done by a true clandestine HUMINT unit. As a result, the information they obtain is inevitably mostly trash, often planted on them by insurgents or fabricators.

The THT teams do not stay in one place in Iraq. In "olden times" army MI clandestine teams stayed in one place, operating from within defended locations and developed "assets" which had area coverage on a more or less permanent basis (Greenfield, 2008). These army MI units then provided direct support to maneuver units, which came and went from the MI unit's area of responsibility. Clandestine collection units *must* stay in one place. HUMINT is about human beings. It takes time and prolonged association to establish the kind of relationships needed to do good HUMINT. It is not possible to do this kind of work well if the MI unit moves around. The THTs are integrated into the structure of the supported maneuver units. All too many brigades or regimental commanders have no sympathy or understanding of this kind of work. It makes no more sense to directly subordinate this kind of activity to an infantry brigade than it would to directly subordinate an air force fighter squadron to an infantry brigade. We used to be able to do this kind of work in the U.S. Army. General Meigs' (ret.) IED Defeat Task Force is reported to have spent three *billion* dollars so far in trying to find an "answer" to the murderous toll that IED attacks are taking on U.S. forces (Greenfield, 2008). His technical and other "solutions" destroy more IEDs all the time, but the number of IEDs planted and the body count keeps increasing. The army likes the present complete integration and homogenization of the MI into being just another part of the army, a part that does not "disturb" the common peace in which army people can feel good about each other (Greenfield, 2008). The only problem with this attitude is that total integration and homogenization has failed to do acceptable work in a war that is not going well.

If the President were seeking advice—as if he doesn't have enough already—there is an important consensus emerging among counterinsurgency experts. The so-called "Bush doctrine" agrees that a troop buildup is ill-conceived and perilous and that continuing confusion about the mission in Afghanistan proved disastrous for America and its allies (Greenfield, 2008). The consensus is that less is more. There are already 3,000 U.S. troops in Afghanistan, and they need more troops to counter the insurgency. A special report on Afghanistan titled "Life, Death and the Taliban" gives more explanation.

An escalation of troops—more troops who don't know enough about where they are—could potentially work against the U.S. in Afghanistan by further alienating the local population rather than providing it more security. More troops can lose hearts and minds if their mission is unclear and they are clumsy in carrying out counterinsurgency. Similarly, the hydrant blast of United States funding for development and military aid that is pouring into Afghanistan in the billions of dollars is fraught with peril. On face value, it would seem that giving the Afghans more and more money to create an infrastructure and build the institutions of governance that they will need could only serve to help a country that has been a basket case for so long. But not all think so.

It's hard to remember just how traumatized America was on October 7, 2001, when the U.S.-led air strikes began, how scary it was to be on the front lines with the Taliban still in power and Al-Qaeda fighters literally arrayed on hillsides across the valley from us speaking in Arabic on two-way radios. We all knew then that this would be a very long war. But I don't think any of us realized that years later America would be pondering an escalation of the conflict, or that the Taliban would be resurgent and, in many areas, taking control.

POLITICAL SYSTEMS THEORY

In the model of **political systems theory**, public policy is shaped by the demands of the environment surrounding it. This can be simplified in looking at it in terms of an "input–process–output" function, whereas demands and support ("inputs") feed a political system ("process") and produce laws and decisions ("output") that ultimately end in a feedback loop informing the input process and policy making (Eom & Sweeney, 2009). In this context, politics is a constantly changing process within a larger social environment. The social changes within this environment produce demands on the political system, ultimately creating competition among the actors (whether individuals or groups) (Eom & Sweeney, 2009). In the context of the Military Intelligence Review, this model gives insight into the forces that shape decision-making.

Limitations of the political system theory stem from its "vacuum" approach; that does not represent the true spirit of the process (Eom & Sweeney, 2009). In the context of the Military Intelligence Review, the process by which inputs were factored into the decision-making is unclear. In various meetings, working groups, and studies, etc., which ideas influenced the eventual outcome more heavily than others? Were the correct inputs or individuals steering the process given more credence than opposing actors? The model also treats government like a vacuum, while inputs are treated with neutrality, which would lead one to conclude actionable decisions occur outside of government. As the Military Intelligence review process demonstrates, this is not always the case in setting actionable policy, as negotiating with input actors becomes fundamental to overall policy-setting outcome. It is also unclear what feedback loop will result from the recommendations made with the Military Intelligence review.

GROUP THEORY

Group theory advocates that most demands and supports for policy are manifested through organized groups and that no single group can monopolize power. It also assumes that competition will decide the most influential group, that compromise influences policy, and that political stakeholders are objective actors who determine winners and losers. This "banding together" of individuals with a common interest (formally or informally) to make demands on other groups in society influences overall outcome. Group Theory further proposes that the central dynamic of politics is the interaction among groups that are pressing demands on government (Truman, 1951).

The clear key for utilizing group theory to analyze the Military Intelligence Review is that public policy is a product of group struggle among a collection of individuals with shared attitudes or interests. There is a need to engage those involved in the process to help ensure that civil liberties and privacy rights are protected. Group theory, however, stresses the importance of groups and overshadows the role that public officials and organizational leadership play in policy making. The military is similar to the judicial branch, which often makes policy decisions where no dominant group wins. The legislative and executive branches influence policy areas that are given attention, limiting the access of groups to a narrower range of decision arenas. Finally, not all interests are represented by all groups. Lobbyists are an example of fostering restrictive access to those with more influence and money, which monopolizes the process.

SUMMARY

In summary, the Military Intelligence Review is complex and requires more study and research utilizing group theory and political systems theory—two key public policy analytical models. While there are certain restrictions to their effectiveness, both models are in line with analyzing inputs, actors, and interest groups. Some additional research questions that could be asked using these models include the following:

- **Political Systems Theory**
  - » What is the extent of actionable military intelligence? Is the process efficient and transparent to the public where possible?
  - » Did the process stay on its given time frame?
  - » What was the decision process within the time frame, and did it meet the overall objectives?
  - » How were inputs from various actors reviewed? Were those involved in the process objective?

- **Group Theory**
  - » Were certain military intelligence agencies or interest groups excluded from access?
  - » How was the information from military agencies or interest groups collected?
  - » Did competing intelligence agencies influence the group, or did one monopolize the process?

While individuals ultimately can choose not to break the law, the criminal justice system needs to be sure that it does not unfairly target individuals of lower socioeconomic means and that it does provide as many services as possible to help offenders reintegrate into society. Through various proactive reform measures, the U.S. can improve its criminal justice system toward holistic crime prevention. This means the criminal justice system should conduct after-action reviews of policies and practices that work and eliminate those that do not.

REVIEW QUESTIONS

Directions: Based on what you have learned in this chapter, respond to the questions and prompts below.

1. What have you learned from this book?
2. How would you apply concepts in this book to your career?
3. Do you have a better solution for homegrown terrorism?

CHAPTER 7

Social Media

The Ultimate Propaganda Tool

GUIDING QUESTIONS

- What is social media?
- What is a cyber terrorist?
- What is a cyberterrorism attack?

INTRODUCTION

There has been a drastic increase in terroristic acts due to the internet. In today's age, the world is connected by social media, which welcomes anyone, including terrorists (Thompson, 2011). With the increased use of the internet, terrorists are fighting a new cyber war that is controlling and contributing to the everyday life of the digital systems through the use of spying, terminating, information compromising, and even information manipulating (Rusumanov, 2016). The proliferation of social media has led terrorists to use it more because of the increased conveniences that it brings, how fast they can grow their platform, and the opportunity it provides to recruit and radicalize new members.

The term "terrorism" has long been debated because it is so difficult to define due to it being a social construction. However, the definition of terrorism provided by the Code of Regulations (Rothe & Muzzatti, 2004) is "the unlawful use of force and violence against persons or property to intimidate or coerce a government, the civilian population, or any segment thereof, in furtherance of political or social objectives" (Rothe & Muzzatti, 2004). *Cybercrime*, as outlined earlier in this book, is a symbolic reference to online insecurity and risk, widely used to describe the crimes or harms that are committed using networked technologies. Cybercrime has some awfully specific characteristics that are used in the world of cyberspace. The crimes that can be categorized as cybercrime have an extensive range, from copyright infringement all the way up to cyberterrorism against a whole society's information structure.

KEY TERMS

- social media
- cyberterrorism
- cyber terrorist

TERRORIST USE OF SOCIAL MEDIA

Through social media, terrorist organizations are able to expand and amplify their presence across the world (Lavi, 2020). Many terrorist groups have expanded their presence in the cyberspace world. Of the 30 organizations that were designated as foreign terrorist organizations in 1999, all of them had websites or another form of presence on the internet. Today, all active terrorist groups have at least one form of presence on the internet, including websites, social network profiles, online forums, and chat rooms that are serving the terrorists and their supporters (Rusumanov, 2016). After the terrorist attacks on September 11, 2001, there has been a drastic increase in the effort toward preventing more terrorist attacks from occurring. Many of the terrorist threats that have been made since then have since been neutralized, but these groups are far from being eliminated because these are global or national terrorist groups (Pedrini, 2018).

Many modern **cyber terrorists** actively use the internet environment because of the many conveniences that it brings, such as its easy accessibility, minimal formal rules, and lack of censorship. With so many people using the internet, the target audience is potentially huge, and because access to the content is unrestricted the communication is anonymous, communicating information in this format is ideal. The flow of information is amazingly fast (if not instantaneous), and it is also free to access this information. In the world of the internet, there are multimedia outlet sources utilizing radio, video, image, text, and the use of propaganda (Rusumanov, 2016). All the advanced technology has influenced beliefs, preferences, and capabilities throughout society and has shaped, structured, and controlled many patterns of human communication (Lavi, 2020).

The internet's cyber weapons have helped terrorist organizations grow and compromised many of the modern critical infrastructure components (Rusumanov, 2016). The internet has become one of the most common forms of communication and has made the world a seemingly smaller place (Thompson, 2011). Many terrorists rely on **social media** to plan and execute attacks due to the incitement of the consequences in the physical world (Lavi, 2020).

With the increased use of social media platforms and technology, the number of terroristic attacks has spiked because it allows them to communicate easier and faster (Lavi, 2020). Terrorists use social media to build a system of vulnerabilities that are often unforeseen and enhance their profiles for online incitement. Social media platforms welcome all members and offer a space for people to find likeminded people and support the causes that they believe in, including political and social changes (Thompson, 2011). This has allowed terrorists who live farther apart to overcome those barriers and establish their groups despite the distance (Lavi, 2020).

In recent years, social media has become a common place for terrorists to display the propaganda and get funds for their activities (Lavi, 2020). High-profile individuals use a variety of social media to market themselves and rally support for their causes (Thompson, 2011). Social media has allowed terrorists to form social bonds with others, share their ideas, form communities, and engage in diverse social dynamics anytime and anywhere (Lavi, 2020). Whereas in the past, society's gatekeepers decided whose voices and opinions were worthy of being heard, social media allows people who may not even be very well-known to share their ideas and beliefs. When people find a cause to rally around and have a sense that they are part of a movement, this can lead to people acting on their beliefs (Thompson, 2011). Interpersonal dynamics are accelerated by clustering like-minded people and dynamics of incitement across social media while enhancing polarization and extremism. This increases the likelihood for more people to be engaged in terrorist attacks (Lavi, 2020).

The high degree of anonymity offered by technological instruments has resulted in an increase in technology use among terrorist organizations (Ceresa, 2005). Terrorists use the internet to recruit and radicalize members for homegrown terrorism operations (Thompson, 2011). According to White (2016), *radicalization*, "as used in this context, refers to the psychological process of adopting extremist positions" (p. 453). They will use social media platforms in order to profile themselves and rally support for their causes. This aids the terrorist groups in political and social change (Thompson, 2011). Many of the leaders of large terrorist organizations have been looking for a new way to do harm but have been opting for the simpler strikes, or "soft targets." After these groups have accomplished many of these smaller strikes, they are more easily able to recruit new members because they use this as a way to boost the confidence of their future members (Pedrini, 2018).

Anyone can post content on social media platforms. Social media has become a place for radicalization, glorification, and incitement for terrorist organizations, such as Al Qaeda, Hamas, ISIS, and White supremacist groups. These organizations upload videos and photos of terrorist attacks that are in real time, even livestreaming deadly terrorist attacks to make people sympathize and draw them to radicalization (Lavi, 2020). Through the use of social media, the terrorist groups reach potential recruits and inspire people to commit attacks. The media allows terrorists to threaten and shock viewers while communicating ideology and the effect of the conducts. This allows individuals and groups to commit violent extremism and violent hate crimes even when they are not part of a traditional terrorist cell (Lavi, 2020).

As the internet and mobile computing devices become more readily accessible to people across the world, many individuals and organizations use social media to radicalize individuals for political and social change. They rally people around their cause to get them to believe in what they do and eventually join their group. They lure in their members by promising them friendship, acceptance, and a sense of purpose, which is something that they did not get or feel otherwise. Social media is a voice for those that otherwise do not have one, including terrorists (Thompson, 2011).

The increased number of terrorist attacks can be most linked to the increase of technology that makes information available at our fingertips. The increase in technology has made it easier for terrorist organizations to recruit, motivate, and launch attacks that can be made seemingly anonymously. These attacks can be carried out individually or in small groups (Pedrini, 2018). The large terrorist groups will focus their recruitment on specific demographics in order to find the specific type of individuals they are looking for. For example, the terrorist group Al Qaeda focuses their recruiting efforts on young people from the West because they use them to transport materials and act as suicide bombers (Thompson, 2011). Other terrorist organizations have used the internet and propaganda to target the youth audience throughout the entire world. They get their message to this demographic through the use of colorful cartoons and games. Through the internet the younger generations can self-radicalize themselves in terrorist groups. Islamic terrorist groups have used video games as a form of propaganda in a way to radicalize new members (Thompson, 2011).

The growing platform of the internet and social media is only going to grow, giving terrorists an unrestricted place to share and rally around their beliefs. If we can better understand how terrorist groups and organizations are using social media to expand their groups, we can better understand how to stop **cyberterrorism** attacks. The reason terrorists use social media is because of the increased conveniences that it brings, how fast they can grow their platform, and the opportunity it provides to recruit and radicalize new members.

SUMMARY

As we learned in this chapter, there has been a drastic increase in terroristic acts due to the internet. In today's age, the world is becoming increasingly connected by social media because it welcomes anyone, including terrorists (Thompson, 2011). With the increased use of the internet, terrorists are fighting a new cyber war that is controlling and contributing to the everyday life of the digital systems through spying, terminating, information compromising, and even information manipulating (Rusumanov, 2016). The reason terrorists use social media is because of the increased conveniences that it brings, the speed with which it allows them to grow their platform, and the opportunity it provides to recruit and radicalize new members.

REVIEW QUESTIONS

Directions: Based on what you have learned in this chapter, respond to the questions and prompts below.

1. What have you learned about social media and how terrorists can utilize it?
2. What is cyberterrorism?
3. How can social media platforms eliminate cyberterrorists' ability to radicalize/terrorize others online?

CHAPTER 8

Domestic Terrorist Attacks

Case Studies

GUIDING QUESTIONS

- What is the common ideological theme that crosses over each terror event?
- What type of grievances are reported by the perpetrators of domestic terrorism?
- What are the lessons learned from each of the domestic terrorist attack case studies?

INTRODUCTION

As with any threat assessment, investigators have conducted case study analyses to understand further how various terrorist groups and lone actors seek to achieve their ideological goals. In most cases, the information found by studying past terrorist attacks has provided investigators with critical pieces of information that help identify essential characteristics within the various tactics and strategic planning processes used. As you read each case study, pay close attention to the details in each narrative and examine the possible factors that could have contributed to the extremist behavior of the person or group. The following case studies will provide an overview of historical domestic terror attacks in the United States.

KEY TERMS

- splinter group
- domestic terrorism
- left-wing extremism

DOMESTIC TERRORISM IN THE UNITED STATES: A HISTORICAL ANALYSIS

THE WEATHER UNDERGROUND ORGANIZATION: ATTACK ON THE U.S. CAPITOL (1971)

- *Classification:* domestic terrorist organization
- *Founding leadership:* Bill Ayers and Bernardine Dohrn
- *Strategic goal:* Focused on challenging American imperialism and capitalism and promoting communist ideologies (viewed themselves as revolutionaries).
- *Tactics:* Bombings and urban guerrilla warfare.

The Weather Underground was a **left-wing extremist** organization that was formed by a group of college students who belonged to the Students for a Democratic Society (SDS) in the 1960s. The goal of the SDS was to promote the understanding that the citizens of the United States had the ability and responsibility to be participatory members in the crafting of public policy (Gitlin, 2017). This group's ideology was rooted in communism and aligned with the philosophical beliefs of Karl Marx. Indeed, the SDS had a set of grievances against racism, capitalism, and governmental control. Based on this period, it can be argued that this group's grievances and popularity were propelled as the Vietnam War was waged in Southeast Asia.

In 1971, the SDS had a group of members that formed a more violent faction (i.e., splinter group) of the organization's political arm, and this was later known to be the Weather Underground or Weather Underground Organization. The Weather Underground viewed themselves as revolutionaries, and they focused their efforts on performing violent acts to achieve their political goals (Eckstein, 2016). This group remained active for 7 years and engaged in 25 bombings at governmental buildings (e.g., police facilities, courthouses, federal properties, etc.) and corporate headquarters (Eckstein, 2016). Many of the tactics used by the Weather Underground were influenced by two handbooks: *Firearms and Self-Defense: A Handbook for Radicals, Revolutionaries, and Easy Riders* and *Mini-Manual of the Urban Guerrilla* (Lambert, 2017).

On March 1, 1971, members of the Weather Underground developed a plan to attack the U.S. Capitol by detonating two bombs within the building (see Figure 8.1). This attack aimed to create fear amongst government officials and to rally other societal members to commit similar acts that supported their ideological goals. The attack involved two members planting multiple sticks of dynamite behind a wall below the Senate chamber (Roberts, 2021). Interestingly, a member of the Weather Underground called in a bomb threat to an overnight operator, which prompted an evacuation of the building, and at 1:32 a.m., the bombs detonated, causing massive damage to the Capitol (Roberts, 2021). Subsequent bombings by this group involved other high-profile facilities, such as the Pentagon and the U.S. State Department (Roberts, 2021).

FIGURE 8.1 Logo of the Weather Underground

ERIC RUDOLPH: THE 1996 ATLANTA OLYMPIC BOMBING

- *Classification:* lone wolf
- *Strategic goal:* embarrassing the U.S. government, punishing those who engaged in abortion services, and intimidating members of the LGBTQ community
- *Tactics:* bombings (homemade explosives)

When it comes to most criminal profiles, there are common characteristics that help define those who commit acts of **domestic terrorism**; however, Eric Rudolph is a unique and interesting case study. Rudolph was born September 19, 1966, in Merritt Island, Florida, and received 1 year of education at Western Carolina University before joining the U.S. Army in 1987 (Southern Poverty Law Center, 2001). As explained by a former in-law, Deborah Rudolph, of the Rudolph family, Eric was influenced by certain family friends that held a belief that the United States government was oppressive and despotic. In most cases, Eric Rudolph's political, religious, and racial ideologies were quite radical in nature; as noted by Deborah, Eric was closely aligned with antisemitic views (Southern Poverty Law Center, 2001). Additional religious influences, which supported Rudolph's antisemitism, have also come from other figureheads such as Nord Davis Jr. Davis held a leadership position in the Christian Identity movement and would make comments that explained the need to have a "lone wolf" to attack those who did not align with the religious beliefs of the organization (Freeman, 2011).

On July 26, 1996, Eric Rudolph (see figure 8.2) traveled to the Atlanta Centennial Olympic Park with the intention of killing and injuring spectators during a concert event held by Jack Mack and the Heart Attack. Rudolph constructed three pipe bombs packed with gunpowder and six pounds of steel nails in plastic containers (Freeman, 2011). These bombs were battery-powered, and the trigger mechanism was powered by an alarm clock (Freeman, 2011). Rudolph packed these explosives in a large backpack and hid the

FIGURE 8.2 FBI Wanted Fugitive Poster for Rudolph

bombs under a bench that was positioned next to the AT&T stage that overlooked the concert (Freeman, 2011).

Fortunately, a security guard working at the event Richard Jewell found the backpack and reported the suspicious item to an agent who worked for the Georgia Bureau of Investigation. Upon further investigation, it was determined that there were homemade explosive devices in the backpack, and an area evacuation ensued. Unfortunately, due to the number of people attending the event, the bombs detonated before everyone could be evacuated, and the shrapnel from the explosives caused multiple injuries and two deaths. Further investigations led to the identification of Rudolph as being the bomber, but it would take almost 7 years to capture him.

The bombing of the Atlanta Centennial Olympic Park had no specific ideological target; however, Rudolph's ideology contributed to other bombings that occurred in subsequent years. For example, on January 16, 1997, Rudolph exploded a bomb at an abortion clinic in the Atlanta suburb of Sandy Springs, Georgia, resulting in seven people being injured (CNN, 2021). On February 21, 1997, Rudolph exploded a bomb at an LGBTQ nightclub, the Otherside Lounge, in northeast Atlanta, resulting in four people being wounded. Finally, on January 29, 1998, Rudolph placed a bomb outside the New Woman All Women Clinic in Birmingham, Alabama, killing a security guard and injuring a nurse. Rudolph was eventually captured on May 31, 2003, and pled guilty to all the charges against him, which resulted in him being sentenced to four consecutive life sentences in prison (CNN, 2021).

TIMOTHY McVEIGH: THE OKLAHOMA CITY BOMBING (1995)

- *Classification:* lone wolf
- *Strategic goal:* attacking the U.S. government to satisfy a personal agenda against governmental intrusion into civilian lives
- *Tactics:* bombing (homemade explosives)

Arguably, one of the most infamous domestic terrorists in the United States is Timothy McVeigh (see figure 8.4). McVeigh was born on April 23, 1968, in Lockport, New York, and his parents were William and Mildred McVeigh. After graduating high school, McVeigh went to a 2-year business college for a short period; however, he dropped out of school due to boredom. He then focused his interests on learning other topic areas that sustained his lifestyle interests, such as self-defense training, survivalism, and the firearm culture (Michel & Herbeck, 2002). During this period of self-development, it was noted that McVeigh read and was highly influenced by *The Turner Diaries*. This book illustrated a man, frustrated with restrictive firearms laws, who developed homemade explosives and used a truck bomb to destroy the FBI headquarters building in Washington, DC (Michel & Herbeck, 2002).

While *The Turner Diaries* are noted to have racist and anti-Semitic tones, McVeigh was more concerned about the possibility of limited gun ownership rights; indeed, he began to see the U.S. government as a potential threat. Eventually, McVeigh secured a position as a security guard for an armored truck company and began to invest money in firearms and land. However, soon after becoming established with a decent job and the ownership of tens of acres of land, McVeigh sought a higher purpose that supported his survival and firearm interests. In 1988, McVeigh joined the U.S. Army Infantry and presented himself as a model soldier, eventually being deployed to the Middle East once Iraq invaded Kuwait in 1990. Interestingly, McVeigh viewed the Persian Gulf War as something to which the United States should have remained impartial.

During the Gulf War, McVeigh expressed his negative opinion of how the United States was conducting its operations in the region. One event, which McVeigh explained to Michel and Herbeck (2002), involved the U.S. Air Force launching a laser-guided missile attack on a bomb shelter in Baghdad on February 13, 1991 (Arango, 2016). The explosion resulted in 408 civilians, mostly women and children, being killed from the attack; many of these people were buried alive (Arango, 2016). McVeigh reported other experiences during the war that led to an increased distrust in the very military for which he was fighting. However, for this performance during combat operations, McVeigh was awarded the Army Commendation Medal for military actions such as killing two Iraqi soldiers and forcing dozens of other soldiers to surrender (Michel & Herbeck, 2002).

After McVeigh returned home from the war, he tried out for the Special Forces Assessment and Selection Program at Fort Bragg, North Carolina—something he wanted to do since joining the military. However, due to his physical condition deteriorating after the war, McVeigh could not perform the difficult aspects of training and withdrew from the assessment. Defeated and morally torn between his desire to serve and his distrust in the government, McVeigh left the U.S. Army. However, once he reestablished himself back home, McVeigh returned to the private security profession and joined the National Guard—a primarily financial decision.

Over the next couple of years, McVeigh became more vocal, publicly, regarding his distrust of the government and how the country was being managed. He felt that all government was overreaching when it came to the infringement on individual rights. Other grievances began to surface, such as racial inequality against his race, that of him being white. He voiced a strong resentment against affirmative action policies since he argued that they were creating hiring issues for White citizens seeking employment in civil service jobs. However, two significant events that led to McVeigh moving toward an extremist ideology were the gunfight that occurred between Randy Weaver and federal law enforcement at Ruby Ridge, Idaho, and the tragedy that happened at the Branch Davidians compound in Waco, Texas (Michel & Herbeck, 2002).

In 1995, McVeigh, along with the help from his Army buddy Terry Nichols, devised a plan to construct a large homemade explosive device and target a federal building. On April 19, 1995, McVeigh rented a Ryder truck and packed the vehicle with enough ammonium nitrate (a fertilizer) to cause an explosion with a yield equivalent to approximately 4,000 pounds (about twice the weight of a Clydesdale horse) of TNT (National Institute of Standards and Technology, 2017). McVeigh parked the truck in front of the Alfred P. Murrah Federal Building, about 16 feet from the wall of the building, and set the timer for detonation (see Figure 8.3). Once the bomb exploded, the blast wave created a large crater that led to the catastrophic damage of the building's concrete slab. Since the building was supported by individual reinforced concrete columns, the damaged slab and loss of structural integrity of the columns led to a progressive collapse of each floor. The explosion and structural collapse of the building resulted in 168 deaths, which included 19 children (Gumbel, 2015).

The Alfred P. Murrah Federal Building was the perfect target for McVeigh since this facility housed various federal agencies, such as the Drug Enforcement Administration, the Secret Service, and the Bureau of Alcohol, Tobacco, Firearms, and Explosives. Based on the lessons learned from this attack, many changes were made to the way risk management and physical security programs were managed at the local, state, and federal levels. President Bill Clinton, as a response to the Oklahoma City Bombing, also signed the Antiterrorism and Effective Death Penalty Act of 1996 (AEDPA). The AEDPA criminalizes

FIGURE 8.3 The Alfred P. Murrah Federal Building Post-Explosion

any financial transactions that support a terrorist organization, allows the use of any illegally obtained or secret evidence in a deportation hearing, and provides the ability for an alien to be deported if it is deemed that they are a member of a designated terror organization (Beall, 1998).

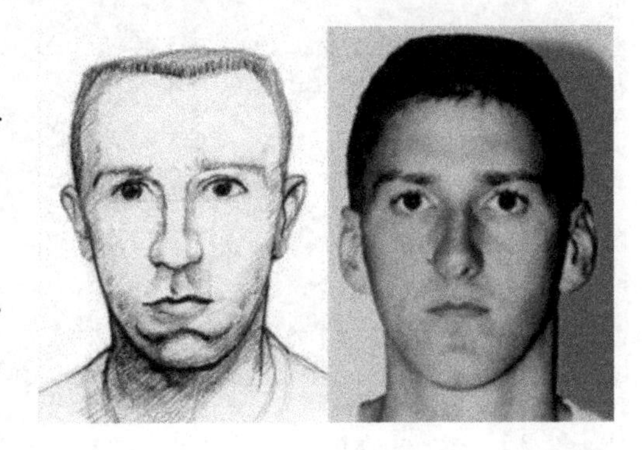

FIGURE 8.4 Timothy McVeigh Sketch and Mugshot

TED KACZYNSKI: THE UNABOMBER (1978–1996)

- *Classification:* lone wolf
- *Strategic goal:* to inflict violence on and intimidate organizations and personnel involved with creating technological advancements in society
- *Tactic used:* bombings

Ted Kaczynski (see figure 8.6) was born on May 22, 1942, in Chicago, Illinois. Background information of Kaczynski shows that he developed a severe allergic reaction to medication he was provided when he was an infant, which led him to recover in an environment of isolation (Biography, 2021). It has been reported that Kaczynski exhibited a change in personality based on his experience of isolation from this event. After Kaczynski graduated from high school, he was accepted to Harvard University, where he studied mathematics. Interestingly, Kaczynski participated in a psychological experiment that was conducted by Harvard psychologist Henry A. Murray where participants in the study were subjected to extreme humiliation (Moreno, 2012). Upon graduating from Harvard, Kaczynski attended the University of Michigan and earned a PhD in mathematics in 1962.

FIGURE 8.5 Kaczynski's Montana Cabin

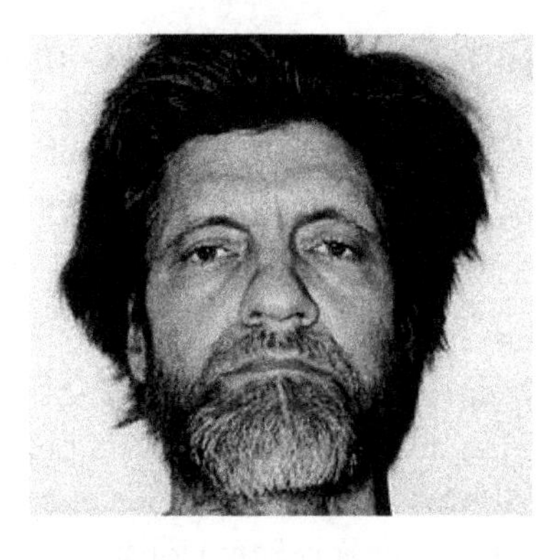

FIGURE 8.6 Kaczynski's Mug Shot

Upon earning his PhD, Kaczynski set off on his professional career in higher education; however, this was short-lived. He was hired by the University of California at Berkeley as an assistant mathematics professor, but he left his position in 1969 (History.com, 2021). In an interesting turn of events, Kaczynski left his urban life and moved to western Montana, where he lived in a 10-foot by 12-foot cabin (see figure 8.5) that lacked utilities (History.com, 2021). At this location, Kaczynski began to develop his bomb-making skillset.

Over a brief period, Kaczynski developed an intolerance to anything that contributed to the technological advancements in society. In some instances, it has been argued whether Kaczynski's extremist beliefs were founded on a personally developed rationale that is rooted in a logical grievance or if it is a manifestation of mental illness. As discussed by Diamond (2008), Kaczynski has been diagnosed with mental illness by both forensic psychiatrists and psychologists; some diagnoses have included paranoid schizophrenia, schizoid, or schizotypal personality disorder.

From 1978 to 1995, Kaczynski constructed and took various steps to deliver various homemade explosive devices to a variety of targets, such as academic professors, corporate executives, and professionals in information technology positions. Kaczynski would craft his explosives with various materials, such as sulfur, saltpeter, ammonium nitrate, sodium chlorate, zinc, aluminum, and lead (Vizard, 2013). Investigators who were involved in the analysis of Kaczynski's bomb-making methodology were impressed by the level of science that was placed in the quality of each device. In one case, it was noted that Kaczynski attempted to calculate the heat transfer on a bridge wire used in the detonator device and how the electrical current would impact the detonator's functioning (Vizard, 2013). Many of Kaczynski's bombs were camouflaged in boxes, packages, and road hazards, which led to some victims being the unintended targets.

Kaczynski's activities were regularly reported in the domestic and international news and he sought to explain his actions through various media sources. Kaczynski had something to say, and the rationale behind his behavior was explained in his 35,000-word antitechnology manifesto that was published by the Washington Post in 1995 (History.com, 2021). Interestingly, Kaczynski's brother, David Kaczynski, read this manifesto and recognized that the writing could, in fact, be his brother's. David reported his suspicions to law enforcement, and Kaczynski was arrested in April 1996. As noted by Fleming (2021), Kaczynski's main grievance was the development and use of technology in the United States; this is a more unique characteristic of someone who could be considered an eco-terrorist.

NIDAL MALIK HASAN: FORT HOOD MASS SHOOTING (2009)

- *Classification:* lone wolf
- *Strategic goal:* murdering U.S. service members as a way of expressing his commitment to engaging in a holy jihad
- *Tactic used:* active shooter

Nidal Hasan (see figure 8.7) was born on September 8, 1970, in Arlington, Virginia, to Malik Awadallah and Hanan Isamail Hasan (Bennett & Wheaton, 2013). After graduating from Virginia Tech in 1995, Hasan entered active duty in the U.S. Army and attended medical training at Fort Sam Houston in San Antonio, Texas. In 2003, Hasan finished his psychiatry training at the F. Edward Herbert School of Medicine at Uniformed Services University of the Health Sciences in Bethesda, Maryland (Bennett & Wheaton, 2013). After the September 11, 2001, terrorist attacks, Hasan developed resentment about how the Muslim population was being demonized by U.S. military personnel. As time passed, Hasan was noted to have communicated (approximately 18 instances) with a radical cleric named Anwar al-Aulaqi in 2009. It is speculated that this is the point where Hasan began his religious radicalization (Bennett & Wheaton, 2013).

FIGURE 8.7 U.S. Army Picture of Major Nidal Malik Hasan

On November 5, 2009, Hasan reported to duty at the Fort Hood soldier-processing center, carrying two pistols hidden under his uniform, and commenced shooting at personnel in the building (Webster et al., 2012). After a responding installation law enforcement unit shot Hasan, it was determined that 12 U.S. servicemembers and one Department of Defense employee were killed; there were 42 injuries from this active shooting event as well (Webster et al., 2012). Hasan suffered a gunshot wound, which led him to develop paralysis (Todd & Lavandera, 2009). This event has been known to be the worst active shooter event on a military installation in U.S. history.

SUMMARY

These case studies illustrate a series of historical events that help explain the process by which extremist ideologies form and how grievances can manifest into violent behavior. As presented in each case, various actors responded to their perceived grievances through violence, using tactics that helped them achieve their overall strategy. It has always been and will continue to be a challenge to identify those citizens who are planning to engage in an act of domestic terrorism. However, if we, as a society, remain cognizant of those warning signs that can indicate a potential danger and report that observance, law enforcement will be better positioned to investigate and prevent a possible act of violence in our homeland.

REVIEW QUESTIONS

Directions: Based on what you have learned in this chapter, respond to the questions and prompts below.

1. What influenced Ted Kacynzski to commit violent acts? Were his attacks purely based on an ideological position, or did a mental health issue contribute to his behavior?
2. What were the common themes of extremist behavior that extended throughout the case studies? Were there any warning signs that could have led to an earlier law enforcement intervention?
3. How can law enforcement and other agencies in the intelligence community help identify potential domestic terrorists/attacks?

FIGURE CREDITS

Fig. 8.1: Source: https://commons.wikimedia.org/wiki/File:Weather_Underground_logo.svg.

Fig. 8.2: Source: https://www.fbi.gov/history/famous-cases/eric-rudolph.

Fig. 8.3: Source: https://www.fbi.gov/history/famous-cases/oklahoma-city-bombing.

Fig. 8.4: Source: https://www.fbi.gov/history/famous-cases/oklahoma-city-bombing.

Fig. 8.5: Source: https://www.fbi.gov/image-repository/unabomber-cabin.jpeg/view.

Fig. 8.6: Source: https://www.fbi.gov/image-repository/unabomber.jpeg/view.

Fig. 8.7: Source: https://commons.wikimedia.org/wiki/File:Nidal_Hasan.jpg.

References

Anti-Defamation League. (n.d.-a). *Creativity movement*. https://www.adl.org/resources/hate-symbol/creativity-movement

Anti-Defamation League. (n.d.-b). *Who are antifa?* https://www.adl.org/resources/backgrounders/who-are-Antifa

Anti-Defamation League. (n.d.-c). *Black lives matter: From hashtag to movement*. https://www.adl.org/resources/lesson-plan/black-lives-matter-hashtag-movement

Anti-Terrorism Clarification Act of 2018, 18 U.S.C. § 2331 (2018). https://www.congress.gov/115/plaws/publ253/PLAW-115publ253.htm

Arango, T. (2016, February 16). After 25 years of U.S. role in Iraq, scars are too stubborn to fade. *The New York Times*. https://www.nytimes.com/2016/02/17/world/middleeast/25th-anniversary-of-us-involvement-passes-quietly-for-iraqis-unsure-of-future.html

Arkin, W.M. (2021, December 7). 'Racist.' 'Extremist.' Did the FBI get the Proud Boys wrong? *Newsweek*. https://www.newsweek.com/racist-terrorist-extremist-did-fbi-get-proud-boys-wrong-1654248

Associated Press. (1985, December 31). 10 members of The Order convicted: Neo-Nazis guilty of racketeering, armored-car robberies. *Los Angeles Times*. https://www.latimes.com/archives/la-xpm-1985-12-31-mn-26249-story.html

Aron, H. (2018). Taking over the state from below–populist vigilante violence and the 1920s Ku Klux Klan. chrome-extension://efaidnbmnnnibpcajpcglclefindmkaj/http://www.hadasaron.com/uploads/8/0/6/3/80637722/aron_taking_over_the_state_from_below_2018.pdf

Balch, R.W. (2006). The rise and fall of Aryan Nations: A resource mobilization perspective. *Journal of Political & Military Sociology*, 34(1). 81–113. https://www.jstor.org/stable/45294187

Balsamo, M., Long, C., & Richer, A.D. (2022, January 13). Seditious conspiracy: 11 Oath Keepers charged in Jan 6 riot. *AP News*. https://apnews.com/article/stewart-rhodes-arrested-oath-keepers-jan-6-insurrection-70019e1007132e8df786aaf77215a110

Barkun, M. (1990). Racist apocalypse: Millennialism on the far right. *American Studies, 31*(2), 121–140.

Barrouquere, B. (2018, August 17). *Head of National Alliance, Will White Williams, convicted of attacking people*. Southern Poverty Law Center. https://www.splcenter.org/hatewatch/2018/08/17/head-national-alliance-will-white-williams-convicted-attacking-employee

Barua, V. (2008). Computer instructions and intellectual property theft. In F. G. Shanty (Ed.), *Organized crime from trafficking to terrorism* (pp. 226–228). ABC-CLIO, Inc.

Beall, J. (1998). Are we only burning witches? The Antiterrorism and Effective Death Penalty Act of 1996's answer to terrorism. *Indiana Law Journal, 73*(2), 693–710. https://www.repository.law.indiana.edu/cgi/viewcontent.cgi?article=1933&context=ilj

Benda, C. (2021). *Dressing the resistance: The visual language of protest*. Chronicle Books.

Bennett, K. & Wheaton, S. (2013). The life and career of Major Hasan. *The New York Times*. https://archive.nytimes.com/www.nytimes.com/interactive/2009/11/07/us/20091107-HASAN-TIMELINE.html#/#time51_7498

Biography. (2021). *Ted Kaczynski*. https://www.biography.com/crime-figure/ted-kaczynski

Boykoff, J. (2021). A tale of two Twitterstorms: The NFL, Donald Trump, and digital populism. In *Populism in Sport, Leisure, and Popular Culture* (pp. 202–219). Routledge.

Brisard, J. C., & Martinez, D. (2014). *Islamic state: The economy-based terrorist funding*. Thomson Reuters, 3.

Cambridge University Press. (n.d.). *Meaning of ideology in English*. https://dictionary.cambridge.org/us/dictionary/english/ideology

Casey, E. (2011a). Cyberstalking. In E. Casey (Ed.), *Digital evidence and computer crime: Forensic science, computers and the internet* (3rd ed., pp. 421–434). Elsevier.

Casey, E. (2011b). Handling a digital crime scene. In E. Casey (Ed.), *Digital evidence and computer crime: Forensic science, computers and the internet* (3rd ed., pp. 227–254). Elsevier.

Casey, E., Ferraro, M. M., & McGath, M. (2011). Sex offenders on the internet. In E. Casey (Ed.), *Digital evidence and computer crime: Forensic science, computers and the internet* (3rd ed., pp. 329–367). Elsevier.

Casey, E., & Maguire, T. (2011). Violent crime and digital evidence. In E. Casey (Ed.), *Digital evidence and computer crime: Forensic science, computers and the internet* (3rd ed., pp. 307–321). Elsevier.

Casey, E., & Turvey, B. E. (2011). Investigative reconstruction with digital evidence. In E. Casey (Ed.), *Digital evidence and computer crime: Forensic science, computers and the internet* (3rd ed., pp. 255–283). Elsevier.

Center for Public Policy Studies. (2013). *California human trafficking fact sheet.* http://www.htcourts.org/wp-content/uploads/CA-HT-Fact-Sheet-2.27.13.pdf?Factsheet=HT-CA

Ceresa, A. (2005). The impact of 'New Technology' on the 'Red Brigades' Italian terrorist organisation: The progressive modernisation of a terrorist movement active in Italy since the 1970s. *European Journal on Criminal Policy and Research, 11*, 193–222.

Cheney, K. (2021, March 24). New evidence suggests 'alliance' between Oath Keepers, Proud Boys ahead of Jan. 6. *Politico*. https://www.politico.com/news/2021/03/24/oath-keepers-proud-boys-alliance-capitol-riot-477741

Chermak, S. M., Feilich, J., Duran, C., & Parkin, W. S. (2013). An overview of bombing and arson attacks by environmental and animal rights extremists in the United States, 1995–2010. *National Consortium for the Study of Terrorism and Responses to Terrorism.* https://www.dhs.gov/sites/default/files/publications/OPSR_TP_TEVUS_Bombing-Arson-Attacks_Environmental-Animal%20Rights-Extremists_1309-508.pdf

CNN. (2021, September 6). *Eric Robert Rudolph fast facts*. https://www.cnn.com/2012/12/06/us/eric-robert-rudolph—fast-facts/index.html

Corley, C. (2021, May 25). Black lives matter fights disinformation to keep the movement strong. *NPR*. https://www.npr.org/2021/05/25/999841030/black-lives-matter-fights-disinformation-to-keep-the-movement-strong

Crane, E., & Fonrouge, G. (2022, May 16). Buffalo shooting suspect Payton Gendron planned to continue rampage: cops. *New York Post*. https://nypost.com/2022/05/16/buffalo-shooting-suspect-payton-gendron-planned-to-continue-rampage/

Diamond, S. (2008, April 8). Terrorism, resentment and the Unabomber. *Psychology Today*. https://www.psychologytoday.com/us/blog/evil-deeds/200804/terrorism-resentment-and-the-unabomber

Eckstein, A. (2016, November 2). How the weather underground failed at revolution and still changed the world. *Time*. https://time.com/4549409/the-weather-underground-bad-moon-rising/

Edwards, L. (2018). *What is conservatism?* The Heritage Foundation. https://www.heritage.org/conservatism/commentary/what-conservatism

Elfrink, T. (2018, December 11). Neo-Nazis gathered to mourn a dead leader. Then they attacked a black dj, police say. *The Washington Post*. https://www.washingtonpost.com/nation/2018/12/11/neo-nazis-gathered-mourn-dead-leader-then-they-attacked-black-dj-police-say/

Encyclopedia Britannica. (n.d.-a). *Democratic party: Political party, United States*. https://www.britannica.com/topic/Democratic-Party

Encyclopedia Britannica. (n.d.-b). *Republican party: Political party, United States (1854–present)*. https://www.britannica.com/topic/Republican-Party

Encyclopedia Britannica. (n.d.-c). *Nazi party: Political party, Germany*. https://www.britannica.com/topic/Nazi-Party

Encyclopedia Britannica. (n.d.-d). *Concentration camp*. https://www.britannica.com/topic/concentration-camp

Encyclopedia Britannica. (n.d.-e). *Selection: Biology*. https://www.britannica.com/science/selection

Encyclopedia Britannica. (n.d.-f). *The Order: American white supremacist group*. https://www.britannica.com/topic/The-Order

Encyclopedia Britannica. (n.d.-g). *Fascism: Politics*. https://www.britannica.com/topic/fascism

Eom, J., & Sweeney, J. L. (2009). *A theory of interest group proposals in agency rulemaking*. Precourt Energy Efficiency Center, Stanford University.

Federal Bureau of Investigation (2010). *Domestic terrorism: Definitions, terminology, and methodology*. U.S. Department of Justice. https://www.fbi.gov/file-repository/fbi-dhs-domestic-terrorism-definitions-terminology-methodology.pdf/view

Fish, R. (2021, December 15). *Reports: far-right vigilante militia groups targeting migrants in Pima County*. KGUN 9. https://www.kgun9.com/news/local-news/reports-far-right-vigilante-militia-groups-targeting-migrants-in-pima-county

Fleisher, M. (2017). *Prison gangs, street gangs: A critique of theories of prison violence and prison research methodologies: Very rough draft*. Social Science Research Network. https://doi.org/10.2139/ssrn.3060649

Fleming, S. (2021). The Unabomber and the origins of anti-tech radicalism. *Journal of Political Ideologies*. Advance online publication. https://doi.org/10.1080/13569317.2021.1921940

Fong, R. S., Vogel, R. E., & Buentello, S. (2013). Prison gang dynamics: A look inside the Texas Department of Corrections. In P. J. Benekos & A. V. Merlo (Eds.), *Corrections: Dilemmas and directions* (pp. 57–77). Anderson Publishing Co.

Frederick, E. L., Pegoraro, A., & Schmidt, S. (2020). "I'm not going to the f*** ing White House": Twitter users react to Donald Trump and Megan Rapinoe. *Communication & Sport*. https://doi.org/10.1177/2167479520950778

Fowler, S. (2015, August 12). *Ferguson unrest: Who are the mysterious 'Oath Keepers'?* BBC News. https://www.bbc.com/news/world-us-canada-33867245

Freeman, S. (2011, July 1). Fallout: An oral history of the Olympic Park bombing. *Atlanta Magazine*. https://www.atlantamagazine.com/great-reads/olympic-park-bombing-oral-history/

Freile, V.E., & Lahman, S. (2022, May 17). Buffalo gunman was kicked out of Tops the night before mass shooting. The latest. *Democrat & Chronicle*. https://www.democratandchronicle.com/story/news/2022/05/16/buffalo-shooting-payton-gendron-tops-supermarket-live-updates/9790247002/

Gitlin, T. (2017, May 4). What was the protest group students for a democratic society? Five questions answered. *Smithsonian Magazine*. https://www.smithsonianmag.com/history/what-was-protest-group-students-democratic-society-five-questions-answered-180963138/

GlobalSecurity.org. (n.d.). *Military intelligence always out front*. http://www.globalsecurity.org/military/agency/army/mi.htm

Gollner, A. (2021, June 29). The secret history of Gavin McInnes. *Vanity Fair*. https://www.vanityfair.com/news/2021/06/the-secret-history-of-gavin-mcinnes

Greenfield, K. (2008). Corporate ethics in a devilish system. *Journal of Business and Technology Law, 3*, 427.

Gumbel, A. (2015, April 13). Oklahoma City bombing: 20 years later, key questions remain unanswered. *The Guardian*. https://www.theguardian.com/us-news/2015/apr/13/oklahoma-city-bombing-20-years-later-key-questions-remain-unanswered

Hawkins, D., & Simon-Roberts, S. (2022). Privilege and the legacy of an insurrection: Critical race theory, January 6th, and preserving black resistance. *American Behavioral Scientist*. https://doi.org/10.1177/00027642221091195

Hamm, M. S. (2018). Using prison ethnography in terrorism research. In S. Rice & M. Maltz (Eds.), *Doing ethnography in criminology* (pp. 195–202). Springer.

History.com. (2021). *Ted Kaczynski pleads guilty to bombings*. https://www.history.com/this-day-in-history/ted-kaczynski-pleads-guilty-to-bombings

Holocaust Encyclopedia. (2020, September 29). *Aryan*. https://encyclopedia.ushmm.org/content/en/article/aryan-1

Jimison, R. (2018, August 21). *How the FBI smashed White supremacist group The Order*. CNN. https://www.cnn.com/2017/08/17/us/fbi-spying-white-supremacists-declassified/index.html

Jones, D. (2022, May 16). What is the 'great replacement' and how is it tied to the Buffalo shooting suspect? *NPR*. https://www.npr.org/2022/05/16/1099034094/what-is-the-great-replacement-theory

Jones, S. G., & Doxsee, C. (2020, June 17). The escalating terrorism problem in the United States. *CSIS Briefs*. https://www.csis.org/analysis/escalating-terrorism-problem-united-states

Jones, S.G. (2020, June 4). Who are antifa, and are they a threat? CSIS Critical Questions. https://www.csis.org/analysis/who-are-antifa-and-are-they-threat

Jordan, L. S., & Dykes, D. (2022). "If you don't fight like hell, you're not going to have a country": An intersectional settler colonial analysis of Trump's "save America" speech and other messages of (non)belonging. *Cultural Studies ↔ Critical Methodologies*. https://doi.org/10.1177/15327086221093947

Joyce, K. L. (2016). Stars, dragons, and the letter M: Consequential symbols in California prison gang policy. California Law Review, *104*(3), 733.

Kelly, J. (2022). *January 6: How democrats used the Capitol protest to launch a war on terror against the political right*. Bombardier Books.

Kenyon, A. T. (2010). Investigating chilling effects: News media and public speech in Malaysia, Singapore and Australia. *International Journal of Communication, 4*, 28.

Klarevas, L. (2011). Trends in terrorism since 9/11: Is terrorism still a threat to the United States? *Georgetown Journal of International Affairs*, 12(1), 76–88. https://www.jstor.com/stable/43133867

Kriner, M., & Lewis, J. (2021). Pride & prejudice: The violent evolution of the Proud Boys. *CTC Sentinel, 14*(6), 1–54. https://ctc.usma.edu/pride-prejudice-the-violent-evolution-of-the-proud-boys/

Lambert, L. (2017, August 31). Weather Underground. In *Encyclopedia Britannica*. https://www.britannica.com/topic/Weathermen

Lang, P. W. (2007, July 1). *Military intelligence failure in Iraq*. Sic Semper Tyrannis [A Committee of Correspondence]. http://turcopolier.typepad.com/sic_semper_tyrannis/2007/07/military-intell.html

Latiff, R. H. (2018). *Future war: Preparing for the new global battlefield*. Vintage.

Lavi, M. (2020). DO PLATFORMS KILL? *Harvard Journal of Law and Public Policy, 43*(2), 477–573. http://library.keystone.edu:2048/login?url=https://www.proquest.com/scholarly-journals/do-platforms-kill/docview/2415857024/se-2?accountid=27794

Leander, N. P., Kreienkamp, J., Agostini, M., Stroebe, W., Gordijn, E. H., & Kruglanski, A. W. (2020). Biased hate crime perceptions can reveal supremacist sympathies. *Proceedings of the National Academy of Sciences, 117*(32), 19072–19079.

Lewis, J. E. (2004, May 18). *Testimony before the Senate Judiciary Committee*. Federal Bureau of Investigation. https://archives.fbi.gov/archives/news/testimony/animal-rights-extremism-and-ecoterrorism

Lewis, R. (2018, October 7). What actually is a belief? And why is it so hard to change? *Psychology Today*. https://www.psychologytoday.com/us/blog/findingpurpose/201810/what-actually-is-belief-and-why-is-it-so-hard-change

Loadenthal, M. (2014). Eco-terrorism? countering dominant narratives of securitization: A critical, quantitative history of the Earth Liberation Front (1996–2009). *Perspectives on Terrorism, 8*(3), 16–50. https://libraryaccess.kings.edu:2299/stable/pdf/26297171.pdf?refreqid=fastly-default%3Afb70e1388ec05db9304275523415344b&ab_segments=0%2Fbasic_search_gsv2%2Fcontrol&origin=search-results

Lokay, A., Robinson, K., & Crenshaw, M. (2021). The oath keepers. *Dynamics of Asymmetric Conflict, 14*(2), 160–178.

Lukacs, J. (2022, April 26). *Adolf Hitler: Dictator of Germany*. Britannica. https://www.britannica.com/biography/Adolf-Hitler/Rise-to-power

Malcolm, A. H. (1984, June 20). Outspoken talk show host slain outside Denver home. *The New York Times*. https://www.nytimes.com/1984/06/20/us/outspoken-talk-show-host-slain-outside-denver-home.html

Makela, M. (2016, October 8). Transcript: Donald Trump's taped comments about women. *The New York Times*. https://www.nytimes.com/2016/10/08/us/donald-trump-tape-transcript.html

McChristian, J. A. (1974). *The role of military intelligence, 1965–1967*. Government Printing Office.

McClary, D. C. (2006, December 6). *Robert Jay Mathews, founder of the white supremacist group The Order, is killed during an FBI siege on Whidbey Island on December 8, 1984*. Historylink.org. https://www.historylink.org/File/7921

McKee, S. (2022, February 1). *Looking back: The night eco-terrorists attacked a Colorado ski resort 'for the lynx.'* Out There Colorado. https://www.outtherecolorado.com/features/looking-back-the-night-ecoterrorists-attacked-a-colorado-ski-resort-for-the-lynx/article_8d8d90b4-d751-5848-97f6-cab9f72f66ef.html

Michel, L., & Herbeck, D. (2002). *American terrorist*. First Avon Books.

Michael, G. (2006). Rahowa! A history of the world church of the creator. *Terrorism and Political Violence, 18*(4), 561–583.

Moreno, J. (2012, May 25). Harvard's experiment on the Unabomber, class of '62. *Psychology Today*. https://www.psychologytoday.com/us/blog/impromptu-man/201205/harvards-experiment-the-unabomber-class-62

National Institute of Standards and Technology. (2017, January 12). *Oklahoma City bombing 1995*. U.S. Department of Commerce. https://www.nist.gov/el/oklahoma-city-bombing-1995

Newton, J., & O'Neill, A. W. (1993, July 16). Alleged white supremacists seized in assassination plots: Crime: Rodney King, First A.M.E. Church were among planned targets of one suspect, investigators say. Others held include a Costa Mesa man and a Fullerton couple. *Los Angeles Times*. https://www.latimes.com/archives/la-xpm-1993-07-16-mn-13604-story.htm

Nickerson, C. (2021, October 1). *Deviance and strain theory in sociology*. Simply Psychology. https://www.simplypsychology.org/mertons-strain-theory-deviance.html

Nivette, A., Eisner, M., & Ribeaud, D. (2017). Developmental predictors of violent extremist attitudes: A test of general strain theory. *Journal of Research in Crime and Delinquency, 54*(6), 755–790. https://doi.org/10.1177/0022427817699035

Notable Quotes. (n.d.). Samuel R. Delany quotes. http://www.notable-quotes.com/d/delany_samuel_r.html#:~:text=Words%20mean%20things.,is%20one%20kind%20of%20magic.

Odom, W. E. (2003). *Fixing intelligence, solutions for America's security*. Yale University.

Oroszi, T. L., & Ellis, D. H. (2019). *The American terrorist: Everything you need to know to be a subject matter expert*. Greylander Press, LLC.

Oxford University Press. (n.d.). *Overview terrorism*. https://www.oxfordreference.com/view/10.1093/oi/authority.20110803103209420

Packer, T. (2022). Guns, torches and badges: The 1979 Greensboro Massacre, the Charlottesville Unite the Right Rally, and the lasting impacts of racial violence on Black and anti-racist communities. *Souls, 22*(2–4), 141–159.

Pascus, B. (2019, August 10). *What is "domestic terrorism" and what can the law do about it?* CBS News. https://www.cbsnews.com/news/what-is-domestic-terrorism-understanding-law-and-fbi-definitions-terrorist-activity-in-the-united-states/

Pedrini, C. (2018). Imagining a shift toward serial terrorism [Doctoral dissertation, Naval Postgraduate School]. Proquest Dissertations and Theses Global. https://www.proquest.com/docview/2206261126

Pelz, M. E., Marquart, J. W., & Pelz, C. T. (2016). Right-wing extremism in the Texas prisons: The rise and fall of the Aryan Brotherhood of Texas. *The Prison Journal, 71*(2), 23–37.

Phillips, A. (2017, June 16). 'They're rapists.' President Trump's campaign launch speech two years later, annotated. *The Washington Post*. https://webcache.googleusercontent.com/search?q=cache:ZoH92GHL10AJ:https://www.washingtonpost.com/news/the-fix/wp/2017/06/16/theyre-rapists-presidents-trump-campaign-launch-speech-two-years-later-annotated/+&cd=8&hl=en&ct=clnk&gl=us

Pratte, R. (2016). Social identity & structuration: A case study of the Aryan Brotherhood. In E. D. Fritsvold & J. M. Bowman (Eds.), *Incarcerated interactions: A theory-driven analysis of applied prison communication* (pp. 77–90). Peter Lang

Provost, R. (2017). *Putting the "con" back in the constitution*. Centre for Human Rights and Legal Pluralism, McGill University.

Rafael, T. (2007). *The Mexican mafia*. Encounter Books.

Richardson, C. (2015). The violent gang in American popular culture: From pirates and cowboys to bikers and gangstas. In D. Schmid (Ed.), *Violence in American popular culture* (pp. 165–182). Praeger.

Roberts, L. (2021, February 28). When the left attacked the capital. *Politico*. https://www.politico.com/news/magazine/2021/02/28/when-the-left-attacked-the-capitol-471270

Roth, M. P., & Sever, M. (2007). The Kurdish Workers Party (PKK) as criminal syndicate: Funding terrorism through organized crime, a case study. *Studies in Conflict & Terrorism, 30*(10), 901–920.

Rothe, D., & Muzzatti, S. L. (2004). Enemies everywhere: Terrorism, moral panic, and US civil society. *Critical Criminology, 12*(3), 327–350.

Rusumanov, V. (2016). The use of the internet by terrorist organizations. *Information & Security, 34*(2), 137–150. https://doi.org/10.11610/isij.3409

Southern Poverty Law Center. (2001). *Deborah Rudolph speaks out about her former brother-in-law, Olympic Park bomber Eric Robert Rudolph*. https://www.splcenter.org/fighting-hate/intelligence-report/2001/deborah-rudolph-speaks-out-about-her-former-brother-law-olympic-park-bomber-eric-robert

Southern Poverty Law Center. (n.d.-a). *Aryan Nations*. https://www.splcenter.org/fighting-hate/extremist-files/group/aryan-nations

Southern Poverty Law Center. (n.d.-b). *Creativity Movement*. https://www.splcenter.org/fighting-hate/extremist-files/group/creativity-movement-0

Southern Poverty Law Center. (n.d.-c). *National Alliance*. https://www.splcenter.org/fighting-hate/extremist-files/group/national-alliance

Southern Poverty Law Center. (n.d.-d). *Oath Keepers*. https://www.splcenter.org/fighting-hate/extremist-files/group/oath-keepers

Texas Prisoners Support Network. (n.d.). *Gang Renunciation and Disassociation "GRAD" Program*. http://brokenchains.us/AdSeg/grad.html

Thompson, R. L. (2011). Radicalization and the use of social media. *Journal of Strategic Security, 4*(4), 167–190. https://doi.org/10.5038/1944-0472.4.4.8

Tichý, L., & Eichler, J. (2018). Terrorist attacks on the energy sector: The case of Al Qaeda and the Islamic state. *Studies in Conflict & Terrorism, 41*(6), 450–473.

Todd, B., & Lavandera, E. (2009, November 13). *Alleged Fort Hood shooter paralyzed from waist down, lawyer says*. CNN.

Trautman, L.J. (2017). Grab 'em by the emoluments: The crumbling ethical foundation of Donald Trump's presidency. *Connecticut Public Interest Law Journal, 17*, pg. 169.

Truman, D. B. (1951). *The governmental process; political interests and public opinion*. Alfred A. Knopf.

United Nations Office on Drugs and Crime. (2016). *Global report on trafficking in persons*. https://www.unodc.org/documents/data-and-analysis/glotip/2016_Global_Report_on_Trafficking_in_Persons.pdf

U-S-History.com. (n.d.). *Military intelligence—Revolution to First World War*. http://www.u-s-history.com/pages/h1694.html

Villeneuve, D. (Director). (2015). *Sicario* [Film]. Black Label Media & Thunder Road.

Vizard, F. (2013, April 2). Matching wits with the Unabomber: The inside story of how an elite bomb squad dismantled the Unabomber's last deadly device. *Popular Science*. https://www.popsci.com/technology/article/2013-04/matching-wits-unabomber/

Webster, W., Steel, A., & Winter, D. (2012). *Final report of the William H. Webster Commission on the Federal Bureau of Investigation, counterterrorism intelligence, and the events at Fort Hood, Texas on November 5, 2009*. Federal Bureau of Investigation. https://www.hsdl.org/?abstract&did=717443

White, J. R. (2016). *Terrorism and homeland security*. Cengage Learning.

Wilgoren, J. (2003, January 9). White supremacist is held in ordering judge's death. *The New York Times*. https://www.nytimes.com/2003/01/09/us/white-supremacist-is-held-in-ordering-judge-s-death.html

Wilson, J., & Flanagan, A. (2022, May 17). The racist 'great replacement' conspiracy theory explained. *Southern Poverty Law Center*. https://www.splcenter.org/hatewatch/2022/05/17/racist-great-replacement-conspiracy-theory-explained

Wilson, J. (2018, November 19). FBI now classifies far-right Proud Boys as 'extremist group', documents say. *The Guardian*. https://www.theguardian.com/world/2018/nov/19/proud-boys-fbi-classification-extremist-group-white-nationalism-report

Winter, E. (2015, May 8). Emotional ideologies: Why emotions and not rationality govern our voting behavior. *Psychology Today*. https://www.psychologytoday.com/us/blog/feeling-smart/201505/emotional-ideologies

Wolcott, R. J. (2017, February 23). Ecoterrorist admits firebombing M.S.U. 25 years ago. *Detroit Free Press*. https://www.freep.com/story/news/local/michigan/2017/02/23/ecoterrorist-rodney-coronado-firebombing-msu/98295732/

Word, R. (1992, July 29). *Jury convict's white supremacist in Black sailor's death*. AP News. https://apnews.com/article/dc459cbdedacf2622b4e9b6e7cd76dbb

Yeager, D. (2021, July 8). *Human sex trafficking of LGBTQ juveniles: A brief for law enforcement professionals*. Medium. https://daleyeagerseraph.medium.com/sex-trafficking-of-lgbtq-juveniles-8fa04d7e3e95

Youngblood, M. (2020, July 31). Extremist ideology as a complex contagion: The spread of far-right radicalization in the United States between 2005 and 2017. *Humanities and Social Sciences Communications*, 7(49), 1–10. https://doi.org/10.1057/s41599-020-00546-3

Yousef, O. (2021, September 29). *After arrests and setbacks, far-right Proud Boys press new ambitions*. NPR. https://www.npr.org/2021/09/29/1041121327/despite-arrests-and-setbacks-far-right-proud-boys-press-new-ambitions

About the Authors

Robert M. Brzenchek, founder of the Brzenchek Foundation Corp, obtained his PhD in Public Service Leadership and Criminal Justice from Capella University. His dissertation research focused on police work with gangs and was entitled *The Lived Experiences of Gang Unit Officers in Their Police Missions*. Mr. Brzenchek's career affords him a unique perspective on the development of policy and procedure; he has served as a law enforcement officer in Washington, D.C., military member in the intelligence community, emergency management specialist at both state and federal levels, UAV instructor, and higher education administrator. Mr. Brzenchek has conducted multiple gang situational awareness presentations, notably to International Fellows at the National Defense University in Washington, D.C. Also, he has met with multiple officials, including the Jamaican Ministry of Defense, to discuss solutions to their gun and gang violence issues. In addition, Mr. Brzenchek conducted a social and cultural awareness presentation for the Marines 3D Civil Affairs Group at Naval Station Great Lakes, Illinois. He stays active in the law enforcement community as a Wilkes-Barre Police Advisory Council (WB PAC) trainer, educating WB PAC members who will adjudicate citizens' complaints. Robert is implementing a groundbreaking art conflict resolution program between law enforcement and troubled youth in South Florida, Philadelphia, and Chicago via his foundation and stakeholders. His experience translates into a useful informational tool for both the academia and professional sectors.

Sean Blinn joined the Department of Criminal Justice and Sociology at King's College in 2011. He received his B.A. in Criminal Justice and Sociology from King's College in 2010, his M.S. in Human Resources from the University of Scranton in 2014, his M.A. in Criminal Justice from Penn State in 2015, and his doctorate in Criminal Justice from California University of Pennsylvania in 2019. His research interests include terrorism, corrections, and correctional policy, with a specific emphasis on mental health illness treatment in a correctional setting, including the analysis of how criminal justice organizations interact with all community stakeholders. Dr. Blinn served in the U.S. Army from 1996 to 2016, first as a military police officer, and then he received a direct commission for the Armor Branch. He has deployed to various parts of the world in support of Operation Southern Watch (Kuwait), Operation Desert Fox (Kuwait), Operation Brightstar (Egypt), Operation Enduring Freedom (Kosovo),

Operation Iraqi Freedom (Iraq), and Operations Enduring Freedom (Kuwait). He has also performed duties as an antiterrorism officer and a customs enforcement officer. Dr. Blinn's professional background has been heavily involved in social services and criminal justice. He has held positions such as Investigative Research Specialist for the U.S. Marshals Service, Corrections Officer for the Federal Bureau of Prisons, Income Maintenance Caseworker for the Pennsylvania Department of Human Services, and Adjudicator for the Pennsylvania Bureau of Disability Determination.

Printed in the USA
CPSIA information can be obtained
at www.ICGtesting.com
LVHW080930250823
756178LV00015B/1264

9 781793 566584